sidney j parnes

the magic of your mind

Published By
The Creative Education Foundation, Inc.
in association with
Bearly Limited

Contents

Foreword

People who deliberately set out to strengthen their physical powers, at any age, usually accomplish significant increases in those abilities — they lift heavier weights, play better tennis, hit golf balls more accurately, jog much further or swim additional pool lengths easily. What would happen if each of us applied a similar deliberate effort towards strengthening our mental powers in approaching situations creatively? Many would lift heavier burdens from society's shoulders, play better roles in life as parents, leaders, citizens, etc., hit more home runs with opportunities that are met, jog further along the road of personal satisfaction or swim more easily towards effective solutions to tough problems.

This book explains how any individual or group can apply a deliberate effort to enhance creative outputs. It tells how to push beyond our present mental limits; how to embrace new ways of thinking; how to excite the imaginative brain cells in everyone's head; in short, how to stretch beyond conventional thinking to the new frontiers of creative thought. It is applicable to traditional challenges everyone faces such as progressing in a career, seeking a happy marriage, making money, handling retirement, or dealing with a death in the family. It can be applied to the more exotic problems associated with space exploration, pollution abatement, poverty alleviation, ocean mining, crime control, energy depletion or health maintenance. Most important, with adequate practice it not only works in the immediate sense, but ultimately yields a healthy and happy way of life for those who choose it for their own.

The approaches in this book have evolved from contributions over the years from many researchers and practitioners. Most of the contributors have worked with the author, Sid Parnes, in exploring the many facets of the creativity process. These approaches have been used repeatedly by Sid in more than 1,000 workshops conducted throughout the nation and abroad. Participants ran the gamut from business people to educators and government personnel, scientists to artists, military officers to church groups, high school students to Ph.D.'s — from all disciplines and callings. He now captures in these pages the very best that his constant research, development and experience have produced.

The Magic of Your Mind is meant to help anyone, no matter how creative, to balance his or her imagination and judgment. Many readers will understand for the first time something about how ideas materialize and develop. By using the approaches presented here, the production of ideas can be made more deliberate and consistent. As a result, individuals will find increasing occasions when Ahas occur — those enlightening breakthroughs when new associations, new perspectives, new insights are born. Readers can learn to better understand and utilize their own creative potential, as well as to nurture creative productivity in other individuals and groups.

Best of all, the book is arranged in a format that allows selective study and practice, responsive to the interests and experience of each reader. Also, its arrangement and content are designed for total brain stimulation.

More creative approaches to the infinite variety of situations encountered in life yield excitement, achievement and personal satisfaction. The creative sensing, formulating and judging of actions to be taken gives satisfaction to the individuals and yields benefits to organizations with which the individuals associate.

My own organization benefited from reduced operating costs, better efficiency in responding to inquiries and increased effectiveness in our training services program — because individuals used creative approaches. For example, we reduced the average time it takes to respond to public requests for public documents from two weeks to two days by cooperating with the rehabilitation program for federal prisoners. We produced self-contained study manuals so business owners could improve their skills as their busy schedules allowed, and we enjoyed an overwhelming response — five times the most optimistic level of demand that was projected.

Creative breakthroughs such as these help keep the organization viable and the individual contributors healthy and valued. The contents of this book show clearly how all individuals can purposely change the impact they have on all kinds of situations by displaying the more creative approaches that make life fun-filled and productive. I urge readers to begin doing this by engaging themselves fully in this book.

Bruce G. Whiting
U.S. Small Business Administration

(Bruce G. Whiting currently is Director of Program Delivery, Office of the Associate Administrator for Management Assistance, at the U.S. Small Business Administration in Washington, DC. The views he has expressed are his own and should not be construed as representing those of the SBA or the Federal Government.)

Acknowledgements

The concepts embodied in this book have developed as a result of 25 years of association with hundreds of leaders in the field of creative studies and creative problem-solving. It would be impractical to identify the countless ideas that germinated from sessions or conversations with these leaders, who serve as the faculty for the Creative Problem-Solving Institutes sponsored by the Creative Education Foundation at State University College at Buffalo and around the nation. I owe them my profound thanks for their contributions and stimulation. I have, of course, acknowledged specific references, but have kept them to a very minimum because of the nature of this book.

Two of these leaders became full-time colleagues whose constant contributions have been incalculable during our close association for the majority of my 25 years in Buffalo: Angelo M. Biondi, Executive Director of the Creative Education Foundation and Ruth B. Noller, Professor and Co-Director of the Interdisciplinary Center for Creative Studies at State University College at Buffalo. To them I will always be deeply indebted.

The material presented has been greatly enriched by feedback from some 100,000 participants in institutes, courses, workshops and experiential sessions that I have conducted. We research each offering for continual refinement and development of our processes. Hence I wish to express my sincere gratitude for the participation of all those involved in this "living laboratory." All royalties from this book are assigned to the Creative Education Foundation for this continuing research and development in creative problem-solving.

Two individuals in particular have made the most significant and indelible contributions to this book: Alex F. Osborn — the founder of the Creative Education Foundation — whose books I read and reread until they were part of me, and with whom I had the privilege of working closely during the last 10 years of his life; and Beatrice F. Parnes, my wife and professional associate — who has been my best sounding board for my ideas, and with whom I have had the pleasure of living and working for the past 35 years.

Sidney J. Parnes
Professor of Creative Studies
State University College at Buffalo

Bearly Limited joins
with the Creative Education Foundation
in gratefully acknowledging the efforts
of Angelo M. Biondi in the coordination
and production of this project.

CHAPTER ONE

Introduction to Part I:
An Overview

Sure you can solve problems; you've been doing it all your life. But would you be happier discovering more opportunities in your problems?...More options?...Would you like to uncover new ways of viewing problems?...Would you like to put more of your ideas to work?...Well, this book is meant to help you do just that. It focuses on ways to tune up your creative power much like athletes tune up their physical power.

Many athletes fine-tune themselves to such a state of physical fitness that they are able to set world records with their performances. Yet while you may not set any records by extending your mental limits and fitness, you surely can keep beating your own previous performances — life-long.

If you utilize the processes presented in this book to sense what your problems truly are and then to solve them, research indicates the strong probability that you will find better ways to lead your life...run an organization...serve in community, state and national affairs...etc.

Are You an Opportunity-Maker?

Regardless of the way you answered the question or regardless of your mental potential, you can significantly improve your capacity to sense and meet your problems and challenges..."opportunity-making," if you will. This book handles it in a playful, experiential way, constantly asking you to react to relevant humor. The cartoons and thoughts that follow are designed to prime the pump of your own mental well....

"It is written! It is written!" Don't you ever have a thought of your own?

Reprinted from The Ladies Home Journal.

The primary emphasis of this introductory chapter is to answer possible questions that might surface as you experience this rather unconventional book. By way of further description:

Part I will involve you in an orientation to creative problem-solving, including some brief applications to relevant challenges and concerns in your life.

Part II will put you completely in the driver's seat. You will begin to apply researched approaches to dealing more speedily and effectively with the concerns and challenges that you face, until the processes feel comfortable and natural to you. You may discover more and more opportunities for creative achievement in any situation that you are dealing with, as well as new options for effective decisions and action plans regarding your ideas.

Want to Move Faster?

If you feel comfortably familiar with creative problem-solving approaches, you may want to move directly to Part II. There it is hoped that you will gain, through intense involvement, an increased understanding, speed and effectiveness with these approaches. They are programmed to help you sense challenges and opportunities in your life and work, and to implement responsible plans for action utilizing the ideas and options you generate.

Even if you opt to move directly to Part II, you may want to return to Part I later if you become curious about some of the processes that you experience. The processes will usually take you somewhere worthwhile, but you may not understand exactly how or why you got there. Part I will assist you in gaining that understanding, thus facilitating your travels through Part II by introducing you to more of your creative power.

My greatest joy is in turning people on to more of their creative potential — whether they be at the high or low end of the mental ability spectrum, whether they be professionals or students, old or young, leaders or laypeople — and to see them enjoy the intrinsic rewards that their creativity offers them....

4

Drawing by S. Gross © 1978 The New Yorker Magazine, Inc.

In this book we will be dealing with ahas (new insights) and ha-has (humor). During 25 years of research and development of creative productivity, I have been making serious, significant points about creative problem-solving through the use of humorous cartoons. As you reflect on each cartoon, you may find supporting and extending messages beyond the verbal ones on the page preceding it. Furthermore, recent research[1] has confirmed my belief that a "fun" atmosphere, that is, one that contains humor, tends to spawn creative ideas. Laughter can often result from playing with ideas rather than dealing with them only in a logical, analytical way. As you "play" with the cartoons on the left-hand pages, you may notice their impact on the processes that you apply to your challenges and problems on the right-hand pages — particularly in Part II.

What is Half of Eight?

In our formal education, teachers usually defined the problem for us and told us how to solve it. They then asked us for the answer.

Question: "What is half of eight?" Answer: "Four." But what if I were to say that half of eight is zero? Would you scoff, shrug, be puzzled or what? Think about it for a moment...

If you happened to smile to yourself or "light up" inside just a little, it might have been because you experienced a bit of an aha. Perhaps it was a mild "eureka" similar in type, but not in intensity, to Sir Isaac Newton's aha in his classic interpretation of the law of gravity when the apple fell on his head. You may have seen "8" as a visual rather than a mathematical concept. Then half of "8" becomes "o" — the top or bottom half — or "zero."

Of course, you might see something entirely different depending on how you view or interpret "half of eight" in your mind. Jot down some responses of what else it might become as you "play" with alternative ways of viewing "half" of "eight." Then "play" with the following cartoon and generate even more responses. When you finish, compare them with the collection of sample responses which appear on the bottom of page 6....

NANCY

By Ernie Bushmiller

$ = 3; VIII = 5 or 8; VI|II = 6 or 2; ate =1 ; ⅞ =7.

The typical aha experience results from new and relevant connections made among elements within our brain and/or perceptual field. A long-time misconception was that these occurrences could only happen by random accidents and that one simply had to wait and let them happen. However, research findings continually show that individuals can employ processes to help increase the likelihood or probability that these kinds of connections will take place.

Ahas vary in power all the way from a few volts to enough intensity to light up the world. The result of Newton's experience with the falling apple would qualify as a high voltage aha; he had been struggling with the problem of gravity for some time. It was a powerful insight for him.

While super high voltage ahas occur rather infrequently, we can experience the 5 and 10 volt variety daily as we strive for new and relevant associations. And, even these can be increased to the 25, 50 and 100 levels on the aha voltage meter.

Can We Speed Up Our Brains?

We are continually attempting to unshackle the brain so that it can better perform its natural process of idea production. George Ainsworth-Land, in his well-known book Grow or Die, compares this mental process to the natural process of biological mutations. The exciting difference, he points out, is that nature's "survival of the fittest" is a wasteful process where most of the mutations are lost. In the mental process, the countless variations (mutations) that we call "ideas" can be evaluated in the mind. Thus only the ones with the most potential can be selected mentally and then developed, rather than indiscriminately developing all of the ideas and then scrapping all but the best.

You might refer to what we will be doing as "speedthinking." Whereas in "speedreading" we learn to read faster with greater comprehension, in "speedthinking" we learn to associate thoughts faster with greater effectiveness....

8

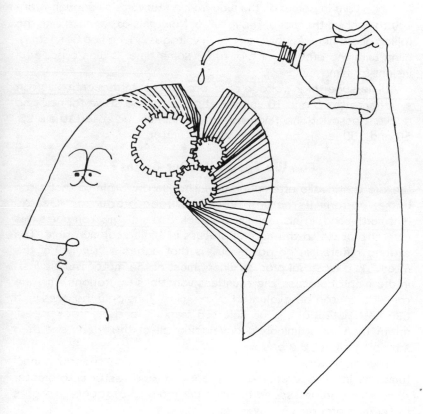

Reprinted by courtesy of Vision in Design.

Are You Exercising All of Your Brain?

You may recognize from recent articles about the right and left hemispheres of the brain that cartoon stimulation is designed to appeal to the "right, more imaging side" of your brain while the printed word appeals to the "left, more verbal side." Wherever they actually reside, both functions of your brain will be strengthened through the mental exercising outlined in these pages. I hope to involve you by questioning you, by providing you with the cartoon images to reflect on, and mostly by offering direct experiences for your participation.

For example, fold your arms in front of you. Now separate them and fold them the opposite way. Did that feel strange or uncomfortable? Most people find that it does.

Incidentally, what happened doesn't seem to relate to left- or right-handedness — only to habit. It is often equally uncomfortable to change a mental habit or set. Thus a basic purpose of this book is to help you "break set" more easily and comfortably.

Growth results from actually experiencing and practicing the processes. As I was once told, you can read all you want to about Freud, but sooner or later you've got to go out with guys or gals! Thus this book is not offered for passive reading, but for active involvement and practice with the creative problem-solving processes.

Do You Want to Involve Others?

I hope that you will introduce the exercises that follow to family members, friends at social gatherings, and work or study groups — particularly utilizing Part II for working together on common interests, concerns and challenges. The blank "white" spaces provided always mean, Respond! Capture your thoughts. Write, draw, symbolize, imagine — any response will do! Group members can do this aloud and/or by sharing responses, thus cross-fertilizing one another's thoughts.

Whether alone or in group settings, the program you will be following is designed to stimulate greater interplay between your cranial hemispheres. The interactions between the imaginative, playful you (representing the so-called "right-brain") and the logical, serious, judgmental you (representing the so-called "left-brain") will be harnessed to increase the probability of better decision-making as you deal with your problems and challenges....

"Foster here is the left side of my brain, and Mr. Hoagland is the right side of my brain."

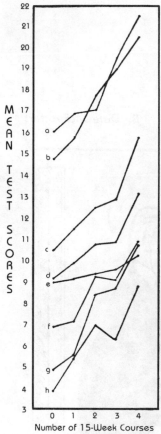

Number of 15-Week Courses

What Does the Research Show?

Our more than 30 years' experience in nurturing creative ability in both normal and so-called "gifted" individuals has provided constant evidence of the "continuum of growth" concepts that I have stressed. Likewise, our formal research over that same period has provided supportive evidence.

Note the upward slope of the growth lines in the graph to the left. The base line refers to college students with five different levels of creative studies experience: no courses, one-, two-, three- and four-semester-long courses. There is almost totally consistent growth on eight tests of different facets of creative ability as more and more creative problem-solving was experienced by the students.[2]

The references at the end of this book provide summaries of our research studies, as well as mention of some 150 additional studies on the deliberate development of creative productivity.

One particular industrial study[3] showed that two different levels of creative producers in a company suggestion-system both moved significantly up the continuum after a creative problem-solving course. The gains were reflected by an almost doubling of both the number and dollar amount of awards received. These results show not only an increased ability in making suggestions, but also in gaining acceptance for them as well....

EFFECT OF CREATIVE TRAINING ON AWARDS

Average of Low Producers

From $33 To $79

Average of High Producers

From $39 To $83

STRICTLY BUSINESS

By Dale McFeatters

"Sir, I'd like to discuss my suggestion in person!"

CHAPTER TWO

Why Continuously Strengthen
Our Creative Abilities?

Let's start out with a brief "pretest." It, like a picture, may answer this question better than a thousand words.

1. Fill in the answer.
   A _____ of horses went by.
   a. steam   b. team   c. stream

2. How many squares do you see?

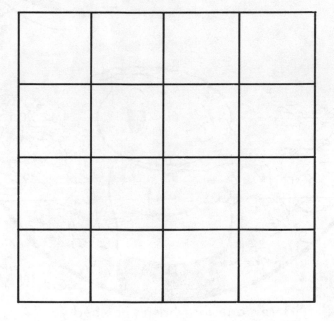

THE FAMILY CIRCUS   By Bil Keane

"Here's one that hasn't hatched yet."

The Family Circus by Bil Keane. Reprinted Courtesy The Register and Tribune Syndicate, Inc.

3. What questions might you ask about this configuration?

4. Think of a challenge in your life and how to meet it.

16

ANDY CAPP by Reggie Smythe. Copyright Daily Mirror Newspapers Ltd. Dist. Field
Newspaper Syndicate.

How Do Your Answers Measure Up?

What was your response to Question 1? If your formal education tended to provide you with a problem and the method for arriving at the solution, then you probably chose "team" as the response. That was the answer the teacher who designed the test expected to see.

On the other hand, you may have chosen "stream," as a great many people do, or "steam" as an occasional individual does. You may have created the mental image of a herd of horses "flowing" by, or of a group of horses with clouds of vapor billowing from their nostrils on a frigid day. How about imaging a few more possibilities that a "stream of horses" or "steam of horses" might suggest?

In your response to Question 2 you may have counted the entire square as well as the 16 smaller ones...Or you may have added the square formed by the inside four squares...Or the four quadrants (squares) formed by each corner set of four squares...or...? Think about it some more...

Might you even visualize infinity as the answer?

One student did and he felt that I wasn't very imaginative because I had asked him to find only 30 different squares. He saw infinity as the answer by viewing the figure as a wall of blocks, infinitely deep, and imagining the infinite sets of squares in the mass of blocks.

Extreme rigidity with respect to the often-asked question "What is 2 and 2?" leads to the simple answer "4." Extreme looseness could lead to a highly unusual answer such as 897 — or any number that pops into one's head, with no relation to reality. But the happy compromise of enough "looseness" to allow flexibility, yet enough "tightness" to maintain reality, produces answers like "2 and 2 may be 4, 22, $\frac{2}{2}$, etc., depending on how you put the digits together."

Can you make four 9s equal 100?

How about 99 $\frac{9}{9}$? or...?

Of course, these aren't the answers that most teachers expect and require as responses to conventional school problems. There we may have to conform to the rigid requirements. However, if we tune our imaginations to see questions in a variety of ways, we will often produce original ideas to meet problems and challenges successfully....

18

Can You See the 'Problems' in a Mess?

In the first two items, the questions were posed to you. Your response to the team-steam-stream question had to be selected from the three choices provided — hopefully the "right" one. In the 16-square item you were free to give whatever answer your definition and method arrived at. But, how often are you presented with the opportunity to make up the problems — raise the questions — yourself?

In the "3-pronged blivet" question, you did not have a problem, only a mess. You had to ask questions in order to formulate problems. What if the problem had been to build the "gismo" illustrated? Could you have done it? Think about it for a moment...

A group of engineers did just that. They used wire instead of inked lines and soldered the wires at all the same points where the lines were joined, producing a two-dimensional figure.

Yet another group of engineers insisted that it couldn't be made. When they saw the wire version, they argued that it was wrong because it was "two-dimensional!" The inventive group retorted, "But who said it was three-dimensional!" I had not placed such a constraint on the task. Had you?

Now look at the loosely defined, "Think of a challenge in your life and how to meet it." In order to deal with it you must become sensitive to a mess, problem or challenge. You then have the opportunity to use your own knowledge and imagination in approaching it and reaching your own decision. Isn't that what much of life is all about? In contrast, much that we learn in the way of specific knowledge to feed back on tests may become irrelevant as circumstances change....

"Blocks, Beads, Peg Boards—They're filling my head with stuff I'll never use!"

Reprinted with permission of Edwin Lepper.

For example, I once heard a professor of medicine say to his students at the conclusion of a course:

> Within five years, about one-half of what I have told you will either be untrue or not worth a darn. This doesn't really bother me; but what does irritate me is that I can't even tell you which half is which!

After all, the atom was taught as being irreducible — until World War II.

How Do We Cope With the Changing World?

The world is changing drastically — and quickly. Alvin Toffler, in his book Future Shock, dramatized the geometric changes we face:

> It has been observed, for example, that if the last 50,000 years of man's existence were divided into lifetimes of approximately 62 years each, there have been about 800 such lifetimes. Of these 800, fully 650 were spent in caves.

> Only during the last 70 lifetimes has it been possible to communicate effectively from one lifetime to another — as writing made it possible to do. Only during the last six lifetimes did masses of men ever see a printed word. Only during the last four has it been possible to measure time with any precision. Only in the last two has anyone anywhere used an electric motor. And the overwhelming majority of all the material goods we use in daily life today have been developed within the present, the 800th, lifetime.

What changes will the 800 and first lifetime introduce? Can you foresee what knowledge you will need five or ten or twenty years from now to meet your life's problems?

Change seems not only inevitable, but necessary and important as new factors are introduced into our awareness. The question is: Do we constantly react to change or do we introduce and control it by our actions; can we pro-act rather than react? If all signs point to our future being overcome by pollution, yet we reverse the trend by turning pollution into an asset or otherwise creatively dealing with it, we may truly shock the future instead of suffering future shock.

We may not be sure what we'll need to know for the future, but we can be reasonably sure that we will need increasing ability to sense and meet the challenges and problems our changing lives present rather than using tranquilizers to deal with them....

ZIGGY

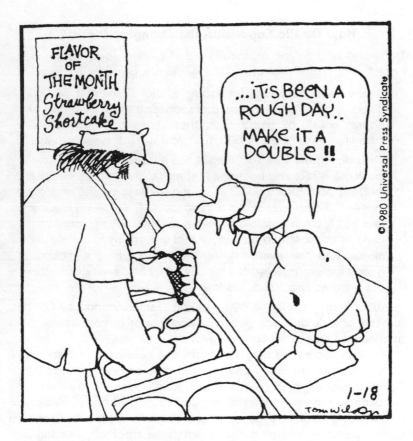

Unfortunately, we sometimes are spoon-fed so much in our lives that we lose the urge to think. A personnel executive claimed that only 10 new junior executives out of 200 responded well to an opening assignment to "look around for a few months and then think of what you want to do." The remaining 190 found the situation too unstructured and insecure. The executive maintained: "We live in a wonderful age where we can get whatever we want; the problem is what we should want."

How well would you have performed on a final exam composed entirely of questions similar to "Think of a challenge in your life and how to meet it." Stretch your imagination on that question for a few more minutes. List some new challenges in your work and life, some "new things to want" — then choose one and list some ways that you can dream up to meet it.

Challenges:

Ways to Meet Selected Challenge:

24

*"Why does it have to look like an elk or
something? I just use my imagination!"*

College students and adults at the end of a creative studies course or institute respond quite well to tasks like the one you just tackled. I tried an experiment once by walking into an hour-and-a-quarter opening session of our course, handing out an exam booklet, and telling students to "Think of a problem and solve it." Then I simply sat through the entire period without saying anything. The students smiled, giggled, squirmed or doodled, but most of them did not produce anything very profound.

When the same "exam" was given and collected at the final session of the course, the students quickly asked, "We'll get these back, won't we?" They asked because they had recorded valuable ideas and plans in their booklets, not because they wanted to see how we "marked" them. Contrast this to the first-day experiment where none of the students asked to have the exam booklet returned because they didn't value their products then.

What happened between the first and last sessions described above is the emphasis of this book. If you did extremely well on the previous page, you might want to merely skim the rest of Part I and move right into Part II as suggested earlier.

Are You Boxed in Mentally in Your Decisions?

Our decisions are affected by the way we view and define our problems and challenges. How boxed in are you?...Are you using all the space you have?...Do you bulge out the sides occasionally?...Or step out once in a while?...Or even move to a bigger box?....

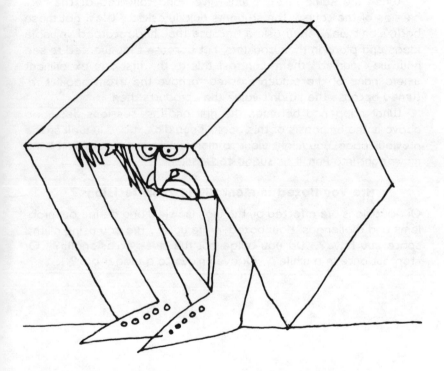

Reprinted by courtesy of Vision in Design.

Can You Create More Options?

Too many of our decisions are habit-bound, straight-jacketed by imaginary boxes. Jot down a few "either-or" decisions that you are currently facing. They can range from the complex (i.e., Should I keep my job or go for advanced training? Should I fire him/her or not?) to the less demanding (i.e., Should I go to the movie tonight or not?).

Because neither of our two alternatives is fully acceptable, we may find either decision painful or unsatisfactory. Too often we merely examine what exists, choose the least of available evils, and act accordingly.

But how can you know what you should do until you know all that you might do? President Kennedy had his own commentary on the "either-or" type of decision-making. He asserted, "We refuse to be limited to the two alternatives of all-out nuclear war or total humiliation."

When you make creative decisions, you avoid putting yourself in the "either-or" box by: first, speculating on what "might be" from a variety of viewpoints; then sensing and anticipating all conceivable consequences or repercussions of the variety of actions contemplated; finally choosing and developing the best alternative — in full awareness.

Redefine one of the problems you listed, focusing on what you are really trying to accomplish. For example, "Should I paint this room or shouldn't I?" might become, "How might I make this room more attractive?" or "How might I save money in redecorating this room?"

"Should I fire him/her or not," could be restated as "How might I get this employee to work effectively?" or even "How might I get this job done effectively?" Each broader definition allows us to create a greater panorama of possibilities from which to deliberately choose.

After thinking up many ideas for these new problem definitions, we may still decide to paint the room or fire the employee. But now it will be a deliberate choice from among many existing alternatives, not a blind, habit-bound, "Yes, it's dirty so I will paint it" or "No, it's not so dirty, so I won't" — —"Yes, he's impossible, so I'll fire him" or "No, he's not that bad, so I won't."....

"About this 'Liberty or Death' business, Mr. Henry. Isn't there
some reasonable position in between?"

Paul MacCready, President of Aero Vironment, Inc., related this account of the way we unnecessarily constrain ourselves by our problem definitions:

I was discussing, with a 10-year-old, how you put a needle on water and have the surface tension keep it afloat. The question was, "how to set on the water the largest possible needle which could stay afloat." How would you lower it and release it delicately? With your fingers? With tiny wire hooks? With an electro-magnet? After a little discussion, the 10-year-old said, "freeze the water, set the needle on it, and let the water melt." Would that really work? I suspect so...the question was "how do you get the largest possible needle to be floating on the water," not "how do you set it down." I had introduced an unnecessary constraint.

Are You Making Deliberate Choices?

We can travel to Europe by sailboat, steamboat, plane or perhaps even by rocket. If for some reason or other, we decide to go by sailboat, we do so with the realization that the other means of travel are also available. This represents deliberate choice from among a variety of alternatives as contrasted to "blind" acceptance.

To do nothing, when there is an opportunity to take action, could also be an alternative decision. On the other hand, we often avoid taking action because we have not uncovered the variety of alternative approaches that might be available to us.

So, try defining another one of those "either-or" dilemmas you listed earlier in a different way. Instead of, "should I do 'this' or 'that,'" ask yourself..."What do I really want to accomplish? What would I really like to have happen?" Then rephrase the problem in a couple of new ways and see if it allows you some new latitude for creating alternatives. See if it gets you out of your mental box. I hope you may see the problem in ways beyond that in which you originally expressed it. Much more on that in later chapters....

Problem Redefinitions:

"I was just rubbing these sticks together and they started to get
hot. If I hadn't stopped, they might have caught fire."

CHAPTER THREE

The Creative Thought-Process: Can We See More and More Than Meets the Eye?

We have increased the average lifespan significantly by current health measures. In a physical sense we are coming to know increasing wellness as our goal rather than merely freedom from illness. But, can we extend the span of our mental lifetime even more dramatically? In a mental sense can we learn to progress along a perhaps infinite continuum of greater wellness and mental agility? Can we learn to tap our full potential?

Mark Twain told of a visitor to heaven who asked St. Peter if he might meet the greatest general who had ever lived. St. Peter responded by pointing out a nearby inhabitant. The visitor protested that he had known that man, who was not a general but only a cobbler. "Oh yes," replied St. Peter, "but if he had been a general he would have been the greatest of them all."

How about your potential? Let's look at a fundamental aspect of it — your imagination. How has it fared with you in childhood?... As an adult? How does it function in your problem solving and decision making? How does it affect the fulfillment of your creative potential?

Are You in a Cultural Cocoon?

We begin life in the shelter of a mother's womb, much like life in a cocoon. Then we break out. And the child we become is a butterfly full of imagination.

But what happened to you after that? Have you returned to a cocoon?...A psychological cocoon?...A cultural cocoon?...Are you now in what Ashley Montague once quipped, "a womb with a view"?

Ironically, the child has oodles of imagination, but often very little judgment; the adult acquires oodles of judgment, but often loses the imagination....

32

The Family Circus by Bil Keane. Reprinted Courtesy The Register and Tribune Syndicate, Inc.

As the child grows and becomes more socially oriented, his/her mental associations usually become more stereotyped. A pillow is associated with "head" or "bed," not with a "cloud to ride."

Our objective, therefore, is to allow knowledge to grow without stifling the natural associative streams of the mind that can lead us into valuable inventive directions. This involves imagination that is not only developed but disciplined as well.

Are You an Adult Child?

"Adult children" strike an effective balance between imagination and judgment as they meet challenges and opportunities that many others aren't even aware of. They see things in ways other than originally presented; their minds produce interesting new associations, not stale playbacks. They make new and relevant responses to challenges or problems that are both explicit and implicit in their lives. Would you describe yourself as an "adult child"?

What's Funny About Creativity?

We all seem to enjoy fun and humor but we tend to limit our involvement with it to recreation or entertainment. Yet creativity and humor are closely related, both frequently relying on appropriate absurdity. Humor, considered as appropriate absurdity, contains the same "opposing" elements found in most descriptions of creative behavior; i.e., the mating of playfulness and seriousness, of fantasy and reality, of nonsense and purpose, of irrational and rational.

For example, take the poetic expression "a lion's ferocious chrysanthemum head." Chrysanthemum as used here is "irrationally apropos," an appropriate absurdity.

The humorist or cartoonist often presents a situation that can be viewed in two ways, or sets up an expectation which is reversed or contradicted in a surprising way. It is the sudden "getting" of the second, unexpected relationship or viewpoint, or seeing the surprising contradiction, that makes the situation funny. No one tells you what to look for. (A joke falls flat if someone has to tell you what's funny — if you don't "get" it.) The humorist presents the story so cleverly that you almost automatically generate another way, beyond the obvious one, of interconnecting the data presented — absurdly perhaps, but yet appropriate. It surprises and delights you, probably resulting in laughter....

THE FAMILY CIRCUS   By Bil Keane

"You put the penny in and I'll flush it."

The Family Circus by Bil Keane. Reprinted Courtesy The Register and Tribune Syndicate, Inc.

Fred Allen observed that the name of the well-known advertising agency of Batten, Barton, Durstine & Osborn sounded like a trunk falling down the stairs. This may seem merely absurd until you say the agency's name out loud and see how appropriate it is. He saw a relationship that was surprising, yet appropriate — an appropriate absurdity.

Most really new ideas sound funny because they involve a new and strange relationship among known facts, yet a relationship that has an element of meaning or reality to it. Thus both humor and creativity depend largely on our being able to see something in more than the obvious, expected way.

You might like to try your hand at creating humor yourself by seeing something in an unusual way. How about a few titles for the "drawing" shown below? Try listing at least one "appropriate absurdity."

You may have come up with Ice-Skating Rink, Squiggles or a number of perfectly appropriate titles. Perhaps you thought up some like, Los Angeles Freeway at 5 P.M. or Circles Getting Dizzy, which seem to combine appropriateness with absurdity.

Like appropriate absurdities, creative ideas often provide us with chuckles or ha-has. But more often they give us ahas, familiarly depicted as the glowing lightbulbs in cartoons. On the next page the cartoonist uses that appropriate notion in an absurd way to create his humor....

Reprinted by permission of the Copley News Service.

Humor's appropriate absurdity becomes the aha of creative thought. It results from a new connection, association or relationship that proves to be relevant, valuable, satisfying or harmonious to you.

Try your hand at experiencing a visual aha. Is the airplane coming toward you or moving away from you?

Study it again. Can you make it switch direction at will? If you can't see the airplane coming toward you, imagine yourself looking down on it from above. If you can't see it flying away, imagine yourself under it watching it fly off to your left.

Chances are that when you first looked at the figure, you saw it moving in only one direction. Then, either quickly or after some concentration, you may have gained the other perception. At the very moment you experienced the new perception, especially if it took a while, you probably experienced a mild aha — a slight "thrill of discovery" of the new viewpoint....

38

Reprinted by permission of King Features Syndicate, Inc.

In a metaphorical sense, the visual aha might represent any new insight we get, particularly when we suddenly recognize something positive in a situation that formerly looked totally negative. The problem magically turns into an opportunity.

Can You See the Positive in Anything?

The optimist, while aware that a glass of water is "half-empty," elects to focus on the "half-full" part; the pessimist views it only as "half-empty." Someone once viewed dirt as "basically matter in a wrong place." Imagination plays an important part in the way we see things.

Fran Stryker, originator of the Lone Ranger, commissioned two individuals to independently appraise a parcel of land that he was interested in purchasing. One reported, "There are dead trees all over the place. There's a stream so narrow that you can almost always step across it; and the weeds are six feet high." The second person, reporting on the same tract of land, commented that: "There is enough firewood on the land to last a lifetime, there's a stream wide enough in one spot to dam up into a swimming hole, and from the size of the weeds, it's the richest, most fertile land in the area." Fortunately Fran relied on the second report, and developed his delightful "Fiction Farm," complete with fireplace, swimming hole and garden.

Even seemingly irrelevant or accidental happenings can be turned into positives that take on new meaning in relation to our goal. An exaggerated example is the story of the little boy who tumbled down a long set of stairs. When his mother caught him at the bottom, he immediately assured her, "Don't worry, Mom, I was coming down anyway!"

Inventor Charles Kettering pointed out that the average person obliterates 90% of the good in an idea because of the 10% bad that seems to be apparent. Opportunity-makers do just the opposite! They focus on what is good and develop it into something great. Their accomplishments are often met with sighs of "Why didn't I think of that?" when observed by others....

40

What it boils down to is that in behaving creatively, we continually search for positive implications of that which is already known
or observable. What we call "luck" is often this knack of sensing or
becoming aware of an opportunity or new meaning in a situation.

For example, a manufacturer of toilet tissue is reported to have
discovered a carload of paper that failed to meet specifications. It
was too thick and heavy to be made into the company's product. The
unsatisfactory lot provided some new insights, and paper towels
were born.

In another instance, a batch of soap was accidentally blended
too long. The resultant mix had microscopic air bubbles throughout
it. Seeing new implications in the accident, the manufacturer launched
the famous advertising campaign for Ivory Soap — "It floats."

Sometimes in the hand-weaving of an Oriental rug, a mistake is
made in the pattern; but the rug is not discarded. Rather, wisdom
and imagination are combined to incorporate the mistake into an
entirely new pattern, often more beautiful than the original.

How About Some Low Voltage 'Ahas'?

Let's practice experiencing low voltage ahas by viewing some interesting pictures in more than one way — by seeing more than immediately meets the eye. In each picture you will undoubtedly see something "at first glance." Then go beyond the first perception, and see
what else you might discover by viewing it from different perspectives, shifting figure and ground, etc.

You may find it difficult to make a new connection in some pictures. My purpose is not to frustrate you, but rather to expose you
to stimuli of varying difficulty-levels, so that they might trigger ahas
of different intensities. If you have unusual difficulty with some of
the pictures, you will find explanations on page 49. Play with the
stimuli and have fun trying to reach new perceptions until you
experience at least one aha....

Reprinted by permission of King Features Syndicate, Inc.

Reprinted by permission of the Creative Education Foundation, Inc. Copyright © 1976.

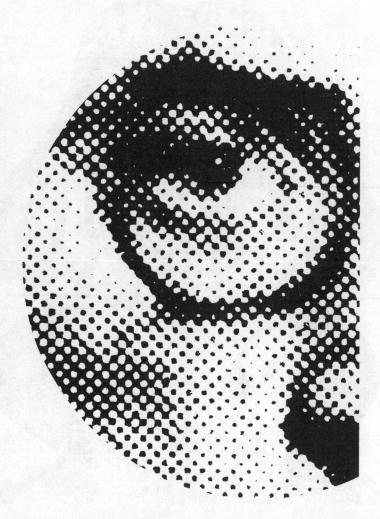

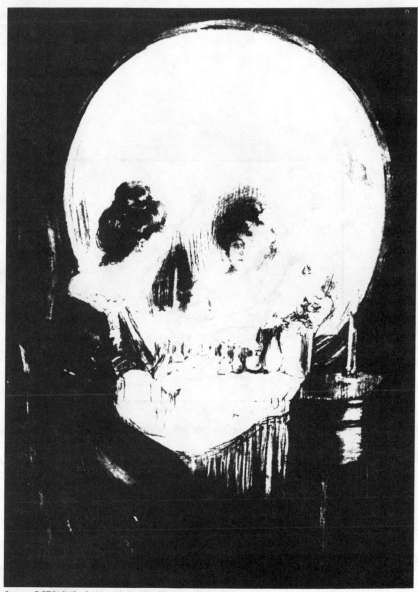

from OPTRICKS 2 by Melinda Wentzell & D. K. Holland. Copyright © 1974 by TROUBADOR PRESS, San Francisco.

46

Reprinted from Dover's HANDBOOK OF EARLY ADVERTISING ART by Clarence Hornung.

Reprinted by courtesy of Vision in Design.

From OPTRICKS by Melinda Wentzell & D. K. Holland. Copyright © 1973 by TROUBADOR PRESS, San Francisco.

PAGE 43
Look for a dog or two human figures — in addition to anything else you may have seen. (Squinting may help.)

PAGE 44
The illusion on page 44 fools us every day in magazines and newspapers. The black, white and grey areas of a photograph have been "translated" into an overall pattern of black and white dots that trick your eye into seeing various shades of grey.

PAGE 45
The optical illusion on page 45 was drawn in the 1890s.... Are there bottles on her dresser or are the bottles actually the teeth of a skull? Your eyes/brain see it one way, then the other, but it is difficult to see the woman in front of her dresser and the skull at the same time.

PAGE 46
Look for a group of distinct familiar objects or an overall representation of a human head.

PAGE 47

Look for the letters CPS in white on a black background.

PAGE 48
The black shapes on page 48 may seem to be unrelated at first glance. They are actually visual clues to a familiar subject. ... This filling in of the gaps between separate visual elements (clues) to form a recognizable whole is called "closure."

FUNKY WINKERBEAN by Tom Batiuk. Copyright Field Enterprises, Inc. Courtesy of Field Newspaper Syndicate.

I hope you experienced a few ahas while playing with the pictures on the previous pages. If you didn't, prop up the pages on your dresser or desk and glance at them occasionally. See if anything new jumps out at you. Or look at the pictures with someone else, and give each other clues as to how to see them differently.

Your ability to see a person, an object or a situation in new ways pertains to all aspects of creative problem-solving. More opportunities to practice will be provided in later chapters.

What's Impossible?

Once we learn that everything can be viewed in many different ways, we may discover more of the positives inherent in any situation that we face. Furthermore, we may come to realize that the "impossible" is no longer absolute. Failures previously viewed as discouragements can become stepping stones to success.

Thomas Edison was known as a tireless opportunity-maker. After thousands of unsuccessful experiments on one of his projects, a discouraged assistant complained that they had achieved no results. "No results!", exclaimed Edison, "We've had wonderful results! We already know thousands of things that won't work."

A group of "opportunity-maker" chemists took on the challenge of making a "silk" purse from 100 pounds of sows' ears. They converted the gristle and skin to glue. Then they extruded it and dyed it, producing colored thread. On a small hand loom, they wove the silky thread into cloth and made a tasseled pocketbook. They proved their point; anything can be done.

Alan Mogensen, in his Work Simplification Conference, reminds us that "the bumble bee can't fly." According to past theories of aerodynamics, the bumble bee's size, weight and shape in relation to wing spread makes flying impossible. But, Mogensen goes on to emphasize, "The bumble bee, ignorant of this simple truth, flies anyway, and makes a little honey on the side"....

Reprinted by permission of the Chicago Tribune-New York News Syndicate, Inc.

Do-It-Yourself Thinking?

The opportunity-maker uses existing knowledge more productively. You may have heard of the chap who was given a rather complicated piece of new machinery to assemble. After a few hours, his supervisor returned with an instructional manual which she had forgotten to give the man. Much to the supervisor's surprise, the job was completed. She asked the worker how he could have assembled the machine without the manual. The man replied, "That wouldn't have done me any good, because I can't read. But I learned a long time ago that if you can't read, you have to learn to think."

George Bernard Shaw once claimed, "Few people think more than two or three times a year. I've made an international reputation for myself by thinking once or twice a week."

Our brain can perform like a machine if allowed. Fuel it up with facts, observations, problems, etc., and it can run day and night sparking out ideas (associations). These associations become the basis of our ahas in our problem solving.

Throughout this book we will deal with breaking old associations and forming new ones. It is the way cells grow in the body; it is the way ideas grow in the mind.

Do We Make Enough Associations?

Archimedes said that if given a lever long enough and a place to stand, he could move the world. Associations become the lever to move and solve the world's problems, as well as our own.

Duke Ellington, like many who behave creatively, was able to make connections rapidly and effectively. He was playing a concert at an outdoor festival when a low-flying plane noisily appeared above the grandstand. Duke changed the tempo to integrate the extraneous sounds of the engine and directed the plane along with the orchestra!

Children form new associations quickly and naturally. And they aren't afraid to express them. Their imaginations often formulate relationships that adults find amusing or annoying. A young girl surprised her teacher who was trying to clarify the meaning of the word "intervene." The pupil suddenly "lit up" and exclaimed, "I get it! It's like bologna in a sandwich!"....

THE FAMILY CIRCUS By Bil Keane

"Daddy's ironing the yard."

The Family Circus by Bil Keane. Reprinted Courtesy The Register and Tribune Syndicate, Inc.

Let's extend the notion of mental associations a bit further. Take a moment and just THINK.
Think **HARD!**
Think **FAST!**
Think **HARDER!**
Think **FASTER!**
Are you aware of what was actually going on?

What is Thinking?

Whatever it was you were thinking about, you were probably making associations by connecting one bit of data to another. The word "think" comes from the Latin "cogitare" (co-agitare, to turn in mind, consider, agitate). Hence when you think hard and fast you are probably shaking bits of data together mentally in your hope of making a relevant connection. For example, if you are trying to think of an acquaintance's name, you might shake loose a variety of thoughts related to the person — past occasions when you were together, associations you had made with him/her, etc. — hoping that something would suddenly connect with the correct name in your mental storage bin.

If you are thinking about a new use for a paper clip, you might associate it with a tie clip and thus generate the idea of using it as a tie clasp — maybe even gold-plating it for novelty jewelry. Or you might picture it opened to its full length and then associate it mentally with dry-cell batteries, as a connecting wire. You might even make the visual association to a racetrack, and then manipulate the material in your data bank until you come up with the appropriate absurdity of using it as a racetrack for fleas. Nothing earth-shaking, but rather a crude example of what is often called "creative" thinking. My friend, Fran Cartier, once joked, "There is no such thing as creative thinking; there is only thinking, but it happens so seldom that when it does we call it creative!"

Perhaps the practice provided in this book will shake up the molecules in your brain, so that they may never fall back into exactly the same place, nor stay in one place very long as you think faster and faster about challenges and problems....

"I happen to be thinking—whatever that is."

Let's consider the analogy of the kaleidoscope, wherein the more pieces of material we gather in the drum, the more possible patterns we can produce. Likewise, the more knowledge and experience that we allow into our brain, the more patterns, associations or ideas we can generate.

However, merely gathering the knowledge — the bits and pieces in the kaleidoscope — does not guarantee the formation of new patterns. A winner on television's once popular $64,000 Question show understood this quite well. When this taxi driver was interviewed years later, he lamented his inability to use profitably the knowledge that he had stored, except on a quiz show.

As we must revolve the drum of the kaleidoscope to form new images, so must we manipulate the fragments of our stored knowledge to form new patterns — new ideas.

Is Our Brain More Than a Kaleidoscope?

Our creativity depends on our ability to interrelate not only what we already have accumulated, as with the kaleidoscope, but also the new data that we constantly draw in through our senses. The effectiveness of creative productivity also depends, of course, on the evaluation and development of embryonic ideas into usable, acceptable ideas.

Here's an example of how this kaleidoscopic notion works in a young child's mind. A kindergartener, who had not yet learned to read and write except for a few numbers and letters, frequently was embarrassed by forgetting events that were to take place in school.

One day she came home and announced to her parents, "We're going to a party, and I won't forget when because I wrote it down."

Her parents noticed the figure "22" written on the note she held. "You mean the 22nd?" they asked.

"No," she exclaimed. "That's Tuesday! I wanted to remember Tuesday and I thought Two's Day; 2s day! — so I put down a couple of 2s."

This is creativity at its simplest level — an example of combining what we know in new ways to solve a problem that may affect us individually. When an Einstein does it, he may get concepts which affect the entire world — like $E=MC^2$. Both examples show how concepts, whether simple or complex, are brought together in relevant ways. This may be quite contrary to what some people call creative where the associations are only original but hardly relevant....

"Suppose we check with the U.S. Lawn Tennis
Association on this."

Jot down a simple goal that you would like to reach today or this week. Set a deadline. Then see if you can come up with one new way of achieving it, by letting your brain associate around it as fast and freely as possible.

Goal:

How to achieve:

Can We Tap Our "Insanity?"

It is said that there is a fine line between genius and insanity. When the insane person can ground his/her mental associations in responsible reality, it often results in signs of genius.

An inmate of a mental asylum was sitting within the gates of the institution. On the outside, a man was changing the wheel of his car and stepped on the hubcap which contained the nuts he had removed from the wheel. The hubcap tipped over and the nuts dropped into a sewer on the side of the road. The driver swore and paced up and down in great distress.

Observing all of this, the inmate suddenly spoke up, "Why don't you take one nut off each of the other three wheels, and mount your wheel long enough to drive back to a service station where you can get the missing nuts replaced?"

The driver beamed with the sudden solution to his problem and exclaimed, "Say, what is a man with a mind like yours doing in such an institution?"

The inmate quipped, "Mister, I'm in here for being insane, not stupid!"

Creative problem-solving becomes the task of finding the greatest number of interconnections and interrelationships among our vast and diverse internal and external resources, connecting them in both obvious and not so obvious ways. The more seemingly remote the relationship, the more the likelihood of originality in the idea. But remember, refining highly original ideas into useful solutions to problems or challenges requires responsible creative action....

"To me, it says, 'I'm creative, but I'm also responsible.'"

Drawing by Wm. Hamilton; © 1972 The New Yorker Magazine, Inc.

CHAPTER FOUR

What Blocks Our Natural Creative Processes?

If our minds are so adept at sparking out new associations — at kaleidoscopic speed — what prevents us from generating new ideas every day? The blocks that get in the way are so numerous that it would be best to summarize them under two major categories: (1) anxiety about our ideas, and (2) conformity and habit-bound thinking.

Let us examine the chronological experiences that lead to anxiety about our ideas. The young child fearlessly blurts out whatever thought comes to mind, with no evident censorship. Fairly soon, however, the child learns "the facts" as adults see them. Whenever he/she thinks of a new idea or sees a new way of looking at something, the youngster is reminded of the "correct" view by the parent, teacher or other authority figure. By the time the youngster reaches adulthood, he/she is usually well conditioned to look only to authorities for any thoughts or ideas of worth.

We tend to fear our own new ideas. Whenever we have conceived really new thoughts, others may have laughed, made us feel stupid or ridiculous, called us troublemakers or told us not to rock the boat. Hence, we learn to refrain from even considering, let alone offering, the ideas that we conceive. I have found an unusually large number of cartoons that explicitly or implicitly center on this theme. Cartoonists seem to have put their finger on a common dilemma facing individuals who want to release their creativity in our society.

An official once reported that individuals who had made very few formal suggestions in his organization showed the fastest promotion rate, while those with a good suggestion record had a below-average promotion rate. It reminds me of a story I once heard about an executive telling his staff, "I want your frank and honest ideas; don't hold back, even if it costs you your job."....

62

ROTHCO

PUNCH

"I'm worried about the standard of our Creative Department, Wilkins — I haven't turned down a worthwhile idea all day."

The next few pages tell it all so well graphically that I won't bother with words. The cartoons illustrate very vividly how we learn to doubt the worth of our ideas at the earliest ages, and how our anxiety over our ideas is reinforced day-by-day, year-by-year, and stage-by-stage as we take a trip through life....

"Now look what you've done!"

Drawing by Lorenz; © 1971 The New Yorker Magazine, Inc.

THE FAMILY CIRCUS   By Bil Keane

1-2

"Doggies can't be purple, can they, Mommy?"

The Family Circus by Bil Keane. Reprinted Courtesy The Register and Tribune Syndicate, Inc.

THE FAMILY CIRCUS   By Bil Keane

"Mommy said to throw it away, it's nothing. But
it sure looks like something to me."

The Family Circus by Bil Keane. Reprinted Courtesy The Register and Tribune
Syndicate, Inc.

THE FAMILY CIRCUS   By Bil Keane

11-2

"You should do better than this in art. I had your
brother and he was VERY good!"

DENNIS the MENACE

"NOBODY EVER **SAID** 'DON'T PAINT THE TOILET PURPLE'!"

By permission of Hank Ketcham and Field Enterprises, Inc.

68

"Sure I want you to have opinions of your own ..... I just don't want to hear them!"

Reprinted by permission of Bernard Lansky.

STRICTLY BUSINESS

"We expect our young executives to produce creative, innovative ideas, without upsetting our time-honored customs."

"*This is just what makes America great, Dutton! You coming in here with ideas and I having the right to poo-poo them.*"

"*I'll admit you're right
if you'll admit you're wrong.*"

By permission of Parade Publications and Mel Yauk.

Think of some incidents in your own life that influenced your con-fidence in your own ideas. Begin as far back as you can remember and continue recalling such events at different ages or stages of your life. Ask yourself how those incidents may have affected your conformity patterns today. If you aren't able to recall any such inci-dents, you may be one of the fortunate few who escaped them.

Are You a Selective Conformist?

Basic to all attempts to nurture creative behavior is the attempt to break away from "blind" conformity, as differentiated from deliber-ate or purposeful conformity. For example, I purposely conform to driving on the right side of the road and hope that all others do like-wise. However, I will not conform to some prevailing notions of educa-tional practice or religious dogma. As one youth expressed it, "You can make me cut my hair, but you cannot make me cut my ideas!" In other words, conformity in behavior may sometimes be desirable or even necessary to a creative life, but conformity in thinking may not be.

I believe strongly in an adptation of an old adage: "Give me the courage to change those things that should be changed, the strength to accept those things that should not be changed, and the wisdom to distinguish between the two."

When we conform to prevailing norms, we are seldom guilty of an error of commission. But what about errors of omission?

For example, on a sweltering July day, I was introduced to a formal luncheon group in a restaurant that was not air-conditioned. This was long before the time of the more current acceptance of informality in dress. Once I was introduced, I began my speech by taking off my suit coat and inviting all those in the audience to join me. My suggestion was greeted by a hearty round of applause. Yet had I not proposed it, I would have been perfectly safe, hardly likely to have been criti-cized. But the reaction I received proved that I would have committed an error of omission had I not extended the invitation once the thought occurred to me.

Errors of omission are much less likely to be detected than errors of commission. If I do not act upon an idea which later proves to have been right, I may be the only one aware of my mistake. However, if I act and am wrong, my error is usually obvious to others.

Most of us, through fear of ridicule or censure, tend to play safe. Ideas are expressed only after we are sure of their worth and accept-ance. We could learn a lot from the little ones....

"Why can't he just go to Sunday school and pray, like all the other kids?"

The extreme effects of culture on conformity is brought out in the classic psychological experiments wherein certain subjects went along with group impressions that were contrary to all logic and reason. For example, planted members of a group would each describe a shorter line as being longer than an obviously longer line. Some experimental subjects, after listening to the persuasive plants, agreed with the false judgment.

Blind conformity and unquestioning acceptance are traits which tend to stifle creativity. When we were children, "why" was one of the most common words in our vocabulary. But, the older we get, the more we tend to lose our inquisitiveness and accept everything at face value.

Conformity reduces the likelihood of creating fresh viewpoints necessary for creative insights. It is the enemy of originality and the creative productivity to which novelty can lead.

When Are You a Nonconformist?

The way in which we manifest conformity varies widely from one circumstance to another. For example, a scholar or researcher who behaves in a nonconforming way within his/her chosen discipline may behave more conformingly with respect to manner of dress or relationships with family members. An individual might respond very creatively to the challenge of constructing a centerpiece for a dinner party, while reacting very conventionally toward the selection and preparation of the food. An assembly line worker may behave ultra-conventionally on the job, and yet produce exquisitely imaginative wood carvings in a home workshop.

With respect to conformity, it is well to consider the difference between (1) the nonconformist who honestly attempts to behave more effectively, and (2) the nonconformist who simply wishes to show people that he/she is different. The latter individual may be better described as a counter-conformist — or one who almost automatically does the opposite of what others do, right or wrong. There is also the pseudo-nonconformist who suddenly desires to be a nonconformist like everyone else!....

"Where have we failed?"

Drawing by Weber; © 1968 The New Yorker Magazine, Inc.

How Habit-Bound Are You?

The pressures for conformity force most of us to form habit patterns that become unconscious parts of our thinking and behavior. In the behavioral realm we do things like shaking hands when meeting someone; this is a gesture which becomes a comfortable habit. We may not fully appreciate the comfort this action provides until we try to break the habit, as for example, when we are asked in a group session to greet people with our eyes rather than our hands.

Let's try a simple experiment. Clasp your hands in front of you and notice which thumb is on top. Now unclasp them and then reclasp your thumbs and fingers in the opposite manner, so that the other thumb is on top. How does this feel? Most people find it uncomfortable or unnatural to reclasp their hands in the new way, just as they would with the arm-folding experience described in Chapter 1.

Most of us find it strange, difficult or uncomfortable to change our customary way of doing things. And if trying to change a simple habit-pattern causes us discomfort, then imagine what happens when we try to change fixed ways of thinking or seeing things.

If I were to present you with a group of objects including a safety pin, bolts, washers, nuts, buttons, etc., and ask you to find a spring, you might hesitate or possibly give up. However, if I clipped the head and the point off the safety pin and left the now much more obvious "loop-spring" that remained in the assortment, you might see the spring immediately.

In a classic exercise, engineering students were given the task of getting a ping-pong ball out of a long, rusty pipe that had been welded upright to a laboratory floor. There was an assortment of hammers, pliers, rulers, soda straws, strings, bent pins and an old bucket of dirty wash water in the room. After using the various tools and failing, most of the students discovered the solution of pouring the water into the pipe and floating the ball to the top.

The experiment was repeated with other students, with one important change. The bucket of dirty water was replaced with a crystal pitcher of clear ice water and glassware on a table with a decorative tablecloth. None of the students solved the problem because each one failed to associate the pitcher and ice water with the rusty pipe — a result of habitual ways of seeing things....

78

"It looks O.K. But how are you going to hit people with it?"

Drawing by J. Mirachi; © 1971 The New Yorker Magazine, Inc.

Challenge one of your longtime habits: try a new way of getting to work, or of expressing your affection for someone, or of celebrating an anniversary, etc. Think about it for a few minutes and then plan your strategy....

One student challenged his routine way of traveling to school. He discovered that by using a variety of residential side-street routes, he could follow the refuse truck route early in the morning and pick up valuable castoffs at curbside. This turned his monotonous ride to school into an interesting and valuable event which he has continued to this day.

Never underestimate the strong pull that habit can exert. A New York City truck driver was on his way to a business address. When he arrived at the street he noticed that it was marked one-way, against him. So, he proceeded to the next block, went around and entered the one-way street from the proper end. As he approached the address he wanted, he suddenly realized that he was walking, rather than driving. Have you ever arrived somewhere, and then remembered that you meant to drive somewhere else?

On the other hand, not all habits are detrimental. Without habit, we would be like the proverbial centipede who got confused when asked to think about which foot came first when walking.

Are We Less Adaptive to Change?

John Gardner, in his book The Temporary Society, pointed out that each acquired attitude or habit, useful though it may be, makes us a little less receptive to alternative ways of thinking and acting. More and more we tend to do exactly what we've done best before, erring less often, but rarely finding new ideas for growth and development.

We tend to be programmed to see things in stereotyped or habitual ways and are frequently instructed in the way to do everything. An instruction booklet accompanying a toy doll is symptomatic of the problem; it began "How to Have Fun and Play with your New Doll." What unnecessary programming! It reflects the manufacturer's misunderstanding of children and their nonhabitual, nonstereotyped way of viewing things....

THE FAMILY CIRCUS   By Bil Keane

"Can we go outside and play with the boxes?"

The Family Circus by Bil Keane. Reprinted Courtesy The Register and Tribune Syndicate, Inc.

Well-Established Precedent: To sum up this discussion of conformity and habit-bound thinking, I have resurrected a classic poem written in 1895 by Sam Walter Foss. It tells it all in a way you won't forget.

One day through the primeval
wood
A calf walked home as good
calves should;
But made a trail all bent askew,
A crooked trail as all calves do.

Since then three hundred years
have fled,
And I infer the calf is dead.
But still he left behind his trail,
And thereby hangs my moral
tale.
The trail was taken up next day
By a lone dog that passed that
way;
And then a wise bellwether
sheep
Pursued the trail o'er hill and
glade
Through those old woods a path
was made.

And many men wound in and out
And dodged and turned and
bent about
And uttered words of righteous
wrath
Because 'twas such a crooked
path;
But still they followed — do not
laugh —
The first migrations of that calf,
And through this winding wood-
way stalked
Because he wobbled when he
walked.

This forest path became a lane
That bent and turned and turned
again;
This crooked lane became a
road,

Where many a poor horse with
his load
Toiled on beneath the burning
sun,
And traveled some three miles
in one.
And thus a century and a half
They trod the footsteps of that
calf.

The years passed on in swiftness
fleet,
The road became a village
street;
And thus, before men were
aware,
A city's crowded thoroughfare.
And soon the central street was
this
Of a renowned metropolis;
And men two centuries and a half
Trod in the footsteps of that calf.

Each day a hundred thousand
rout
Followed this zigzag calf about
And o'er his crooked journey
went
The traffic of a continent.

A hundred thousand men were
led
By one calf near three centuries
dead.
They followed still his crooked
way,
And lost one hundred years a
day;
For thus such reverence is lent
To well-established precedent.

82

CHAPTER FIVE

How Do We Overcome the Blocks?

In order to experience what will be discussed in this chapter, allow yourself five minutes to list ideas for meeting a challenge that you have....

Challenge:

Ideas:

84

© 1971 United feature Syndicate, Inc.

If we are to break habit-sets and move into new, original ways of viewing our problems and challenges, we must find ways to break old mental associations or connections and form new ones.

What Is Deferred Judgment?

Deferred judgment is a fundamental principle that can open us to the greatest flow of associations or connections of new ideas. It frees us from anxieties about the worth and acceptability or appropriateness of raw ideas as we conceive them.

This principle has been extensively researched. When used by groups in the idea-generating stage of the problem-solving process, it is commonly called brainstorming. The term was coined by its originator, Alex F. Osborn, and popularized in the 1950s.

The fundamental basis of deferred judgment, however, goes back as far as Ecclesiasticus in the Old Testament Apocrypha. One of its pithy sayings states: "Think first, criticize afterward." The great poet-philosopher Frederick Schiller expanded on this in 1788:

Apparently, it is not good — and indeed it hinders the creative work of the mind — if the intellect examines too closely the ideas already pouring in, as it were, at the gates. Regarded in isolation, an idea may be quite insignificant, and venturesome in the extreme, but it may acquire importance from an idea which follows it;... In the case of a creative mind, it seems to me, the intellect has withdrawn its watchers from the gates, and the ideas rush in pell-mell, and only then does it review and inspect the multitude.[4]

The essence of deferred judgment is to allow a given period of time for listing all the ideas that come to mind regarding a problem, without judging them in any way. Forget about the quality of the ideas entirely and stretch for quantity. Combine or modify any of the ideas which have already been listed in order to produce additional ideas. Quantity and freedom of expression, without evaluation, are the key points which allow free reign to the imagination. Many of the psychological blocks caused by habit and past experience are broken down by the strange associations that take place during the "free wheeling" process of deferred judgment....

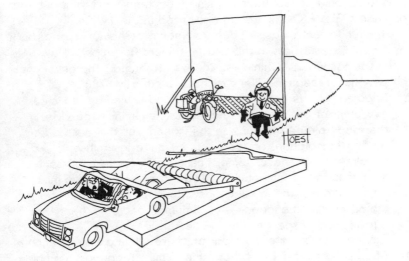

"I warned you about the speed traps in this town!"

Reprinted by courtesy of Bill Hoest.

Deferred judgment involves looking at ideas and seeing where they might take us instead of merely trying to see what's right or wrong with them. The spontaneous associations which occur may help trigger important connections with knowledge and experience that we may have forgotten or repressed.

Deferring judgment also reduces the tendency to grasp frantically for the first idea or solution that reduces the anxiety of a situation. It leads to a wide search for alternatives — alternatives which ultimately provide a greater freedom of choice in making decisions. Furthermore, it can promote greater confidence in the decision, because there is less chance of having overlooked alternatives.

A classic example of the kinds of unique ideas that can emerge while deferring judgment involves packers of automobile parts who were wasting time reading the old newspapers used for packing material. The problem was to prevent this waste of time. Four ideas that emerged during a problem-solving session were: (1) hire illiterate packers, (2) use foreign language papers, (3) blindfold them, (4) hire blind packers. The fourth solution was adopted by the car manufacturer. Note the interesting associative process that seems to have led to the adopted solution.

What About Our Automatic Reactions?

It is often difficult not to have some kind of reaction to the spontaneous new ideas that enter our minds while deferring judgment. Whether this reaction is positive or negative, it need not prevent us from considering or simply listing the ideas. Although we may react to a new idea, we need not make any evaluation during the idea-finding stage. We might even jot down our momentary reaction as an additional idea. For example, if our unavoidable and immediate reaction to an idea is "too costly," we might note, "reduce cost," or "get some extra funds" as additional ideas.

Try your hand at deferring judgment for five minutes while listing as many ideas as you can regarding the challenge that you chose at the beginning of this chapter, or a new challenge if you prefer. Really let yourself go — experiment with the principle. Let your ideas flow as rapidly as they pop into your head. Later, you can look them over and see what you produced or where they led you. But for five minutes, just let them flow, as though automatically, from your head, through your fingers, onto the next page....

The Saturday Evening Post
© The Curtis Publishing Company

Mentally "go with the flow," and see how many ideas you can generate. Make this a personal experiment. See if you can experience capturing anything that comes to mind, no matter how strange or even absurd....

Challenge:

Ideas: Have fun, Defer, Play, Flow!

Reprinted by permission of the Chicago Tribune-New York News Syndicate, Inc.

How did you do? Did you experience a true release? Did you have some ha has as well as ahas as you went along?

How do your ideas compare with those during the first five minutes (page 83)?...In quantity?...In quality?...In potential value for development into useful ideas?

Research shows that significant gains are made using deferred judgment. However, if you didn't notice any apparent gain in the last experience, you might like to try again, perhaps with another person or persons. Explain the notion of deferred judgment first, and ask them to "let loose" with you. Part II will also provide additional opportunities for you to use the principle again in a variety of useful ways.

Would You Like to Double Your Productivity?

Deferred judgment is deceptively simple to understand intellectually but extremely difficult to internalize. It takes practice, like any new skill.

Striking evidence of the value of practicing deferred judgment appeared in a study where we compared novices to experienced practitioners. Both groups were told to defer judgment, relate freely, strive for quantity of alternatives, etc. The experienced subjects, equivalent in all other respects to the naive group, outproduced the novices (in the same length of time) approximately two to one, on both quantity and quality of ideas as solutions to a problem. The results were highly significant statistically.

Artist Charles Burchfield exemplified the principle of deferred judgment in his style of painting. He kept a collection of over 1,000 ideas on scraps of paper. Furthermore, in completing a painting, he would paste over modifications of portions of the scene while attempting to achieve the effect he wanted. Once he casually remarked to an audience, "I don't know if these paintings are finished or not."....

THE FAMILY CIRCUS   By Bil Keane

"What are you drawing?" "I don't know. It
isn't finished yet."

The Family Circus by Bil Keane. Reprinted Courtesy The Register and Tribune
Syndicate, Inc.

"Don't put off until tomorrow what you can do today," is an old adage that may be only partly true. The other side of the coin might be, "Don't make any decision today that can wait until tomorrow." Deferring judgment may lead to new ideas that can improve the decision.

The concept of deferred judgment is clearly differentiated from both pre-judgment and no-judgment. Prejudgment or "prejudice," connotes premature closure that is unyielding to new input. No-judgment connotes total openness without closure or decision ever occurring. But, can we stay free of prejudice forever? Hardly, for we would never make a decision; we would continue to wait for still more facts to come in.

If we could speak of the qualities of "prejudiced," "nojudiced" and "deferjudiced," the term "deferjudiced" would imply taking an ever larger number of factors into consideration, in a given unit of time, before making a decision and taking action. The decision probably would be a better one, according to both research and the experience of those who practice this behavior.

"Deferjudiced" would also imply a willingness to reconsider the temporary "prejudices" that decisions represent, when new data surface. Nothing is ever final — like the sign stating, "That's my decision and it's final — for the moment."

€xtended €ffort?

Related closely to the deferment-of-judgment principle is a theory that extended effort in generating ideas tends to produce a greater proportion of good ideas among those generated later. Check your deferred-judgment list on page 89 to see if you notice more intriguing, promising, or potentially valuable ideas showing up later on your list.

William J. J. Gordon describes "deferment" in the creative process as "the capacity to discard the glittering immediate in favor of a shadowy but possibly richer future." Like in long-term financial investing, we can forego the immediate reward of applying our first idea in expectation of an ultimately better solution.

How about investing another five minutes or so in the free flow of ideas regarding your challenge on page 89 or a new one. Use the cartoon on the next page to help put you in a playful, free-wheeling frame of mind. Let it trigger associated thoughts for you....

Drawing by Nicolae Asciu; © 1976 The New Yorker Magazine, Inc.

Want a Few Idea-Stimulation Techniques?

The deferred-judgment principle might be thought of as the "environmental turnpike" that allows free flow to ideas that come to your mind. But what do you do when ideas aren't flowing? While the "turnpike" concept allows and encourages you to express ideas as they occur, you may often need to use other procedures which help to bring the ideas to mind in the first place, so that you do not become stranded on the turnpike, out of gas (like Snoopy at the typewriter). The following are some of the more productive techniques for triggering new ideas.

CHECKLISTS. In his classic text, Applied Imagination, Alex F. Osborn explains an effective checklist consisting of a series of verbs used to change mental set as one contemplates a problem or a challenge. For example, three of the verbs are: magnify, minify and rearrange.

Suppose a family were trying to generate ideas on ways to enjoy their meals together more fully. If they were to think about the situation and apply magnify, they might come up with ideas like (1) inviting diverse people — foreign students, teachers, local artists, etc. — or (2) lengthening an occasional dinner by combining it with a favorite record album between courses. Minify might suggest (1) decreasing the size of the portions in each dinner course, but increasing the number of courses, so as to provide more variety and interest to the dinner; or (2) eating around a very small table so as to make the whole dinner much more intimate; or (3) eliminating the meal and feeding a needy family instead. Rearrange might suggest eating in the living room or on the porch, or having a reverse meal with the dessert first.

A recent idea in the pharmaceutical field is based on the magnify notion. It involves adding an emetic to the coating of drugs that pose a danger if used excessively — such as sleeping pills. Taken as prescribed, the small amount of emetic in each pill has no effect. If too many pills are ingested, the accumulated emetic from the coatings induces vomiting, thus "automatically" ejecting the overdose. In this example, magnification takes the form of adding or combining.

Cartoonists frequently make use of the checklist verbs to create appropriate absurdity, the basis for their humor. For example, rearrange by reversing....

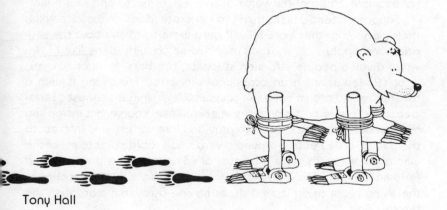

Tony Hall

In all the examples and exercises throughout this chapter, remember that the first ideas conceived are only starting points. They can always trigger adaptations and related ideas that are more interesting and valuable than the original thoughts.

How about trying your hand at generating additional ideas for ways to enjoy (family) meals together more fully, or for one of your own challenges, based on the three idea-spurring categories. Remember, defer judgment! Anything goes!

Magnify: (Enlarge, multiply, add, increase, exaggerate, etc.)

Minify: (Subtract, divide, eliminate, shorten, simplify, etc.)

Rearrange: (Reverse, turn around, combine, substitute, scatter, etc.)

Now choose one idea that you like particularly and try to refine it into an idea that you can use....

GUMDROP   **By George Crenshaw**

© 1977 United Feature Syndicate, Inc.

FORCED RELATIONSHIPS. Another fundamental procedure involves taking anything in our awareness and attempting to relate it to the problem at hand. For example, in the previous meal situation, suppose the family focused on a tree outside the window. Someone might notice the leaves and suggest serving some element of the meal on attractive leaves; still another person might see highly-textured bark which might suggest small ice-carvings as table decorations.

Can We Use All of Our Senses?

Forced relationships might involve senses other than sight. The family might focus on a bird twittering outside and attempt to force a relationship between that sound and the situation. It could prompt ideas such as introducing a music box for background sound-effects, or telling each other how they feel by humming accordingly.

Aside from using current sensations as stimuli for forcing relationships, we can use imagination for providing additional stimuli. We might imaginatively take a safari into Africa, and associate the meal with something there: plan a meal around the TV show, Wild Kingdom; "monkey around" with the way the food is served — the soup in glasses, the coffee in soup bowls, the ice cream on large platters, etc.; eat a picnic meal in a canoe or rowboat on a body of water. I have often stimulated groups that were running out of new ideas by encouraging them to take imaginary trips to one place or another.

Try to force a few relationships yourself now in regard to the meal challenge, or one of your own choosing. Again, defer judgment!

Anything may become relevant; creativity involves discovering the meaning in relationships that are not obviously relevant. The young woman on the next page probably understands this better than her suitor....

"Actually, I'm seeking a meaningless relationship."

Deliberate or forced relationships may be turned on while conventional or habitual associations are shelved temporarily, or deferred. For example, if I ask you to associate a chair with a car, the obvious connection might be that both have seats.

If we examine the forced relationship further, we might observe that a car has wheels and ask, "Might a chair have wheels?" That may have sounded strange many years ago, but the idea is now commonly seen in the form of wheels or casters on chairs. If we stretched further, we might arrive at the even stranger association of the wheel on its side serving as the seat of the chair. From that somewhat bizarre notion might evolve the thought of the seat of the chair turning like a wheel. Suddenly we have conceived the idea of the now well-known swivel chair.

Can You Manipulate Your Images?

Thus, new relationships can frequently be forced by manipulating observations that we make, or images that we form in our minds. The inventor of the fork-lift truck reputedly conceived the initial idea while observing (and magnifying) the mechanism that lifts donuts into a donut oven.

Another inventor is said to have achieved his synchronization of the machinegun with the airplane propeller by visualizing how he threw rocks through windmill blades as a boy. His childhood experience suddenly became very relevant to his problem.

A final idea or product might not always evolve from one simple step, but from many channels of connections that open up after the initial forced relationship is made between seemingly unrelated items.

Think of the car or bus you ride. Focus on some part of it other than the seat or wheel. Now relate the part you selected to the chair you are sitting on. Defer judgment and play with it; visualize magnifying it, minifying it, rearranging it or a quality of it (the shininess of the bumper, for example) until you picture a connection that you might like to make with your own chair. If you don't come up with something you like, try it again later with different parts of the car or bus until something clicks for you. It is often especially exciting when your aha comes after stretching awhile....

ATTRIBUTE LISTING. Another commonly used process to aid the flow of ideas is called attribute listing. It involves taking specific aspects of an object or situation and then focusing particularly on the aspect selected. The checklisting or the forced-relationship processes can then be applied to whatever specific aspect is the subject of focus.

In the meal situation, we might look at the question of dessert, and examine everything we know about it — the shapes, colors, tastes, etc., of each specific dessert that we might think of. Then we might vary any one of those attributes or connect something else to that specific attribute.

Suppose we selected orange jello, cut into squares. One attribute might be that it was "soft and shimmery." If we focused on a brick in the fireplace and applied the hardness of the brick to the soft and shimmery quality of the jello, it might lead to the idea of freezing the jello and making it into a semi-icy dessert. The mental trip to Africa might suggest an animal-carving contest out of each one's jello before eating it. And so on.

Now try for a few ideas yourself on a different attribute of a particular dessert...or some other aspect of the meal...or some other challenge you might prefer. Defer judgment, and have fun!

Attribute Chosen:

Ideas:

Now choose one you like and try to refine it into an idea you can use....

Recycling Old Clothes

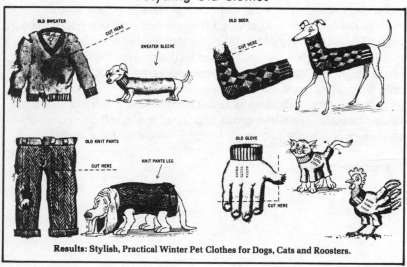

Results: Stylish, Practical Winter Pet Clothes for Dogs, Cats and Roosters.

Reprinted with permission from Mad Magazine © 1974 by E. C. Publications, Inc.

MORPHOLOGICAL APPROACH. The morphological procedure applies the notion of attribute listing together with forced relationship, in a matrix approach. It speeds the production of countless ideas.

In the meal illustration, we might list some of the following attributes: people involved, places, times, foods, special effects, etc. Under each heading we would list a number of alternatives. For "people" we might jot down family, friends, strangers, needy people, celebrities, etc....for "places" we might list different parts of the house, outdoors, picnics, campgrounds, etc....for "times" we might list breakfast, lunch, dinner, snack-time, etc....for "foods" we could list all kinds of different food items...for "special effects" we might have music, TV, odors, incense, etc.

Then we would take items at random from each of the headings (attributes) and connect them into a novel meal idea. For example, we might randomly select celebrity, basement, breakfast, hamburger, incense and put them together or adapt them in different ways: "incense" the "head of the house" by serving the kids hamburger for breakfast in the basement game room. Notice that we don't necessarily take the words literally. Incense suggested something different from a "special effect"; so did "monkey" in the earlier example.

Now form one or two random combinations of your own. Deferring judgment, see if you can interconnect other items from each list above into new meal ideas....

Elements to interconnect:

Ideas:

Recycling Old Ties

Results: Beautiful, Colorful Table Cloths, Skirts, Throw Rugs and Curtains.

These processes can help us to break away from some of our habitual thinking — some of our rigidity — and to form new connections of thoughts. Remember though that these ideas are only starting points in the creative process. A great deal of refinement and development are usually necessary to make the ideas workable within the realities that exist.

The idea-stimulation techniques described here are examples of some of the main categories of methods used to help prompt the imagination. Many others will be used in the divergent stage of each step of the creative problem-solving process practiced later in the book.

At each divergent stage of the process, deferred judgment is used. Everything possible is done to maintain a constant flow of thoughts, whether these be the facts, problems, ideas, criteria for solution-finding, or the means of implementing and gaining acceptance. Research and practice have shown that the greater the flow of thoughts at each of these stages, the greater the likelihood of new insights and connections that become relevant as they are developed through the balance of the process.

What Is the Ultimate Purpose of Deferring Judgment?

At the same time, I must re-emphasize that divergent production — the creation of many unevaluated alternatives at each stage — is not an end in itself, but only a means to an end. Ultimately, judgment re-enters the scene, facilitating convergence, solution and effective decision making — the ultimate purpose of the creative process.

What we are attempting to do is to get data out of memory storage and relate it to the current situation. So much of our problem-solving relies on data that is stored deep within us, data that we don't have in our present awareness and therefore fail to connect with the present situation. If we enable more of this data from memory storage to surface into our awareness, we are more likely to make rewarding connections. It is a "probability game" with no guarantees, but we are doing what Nobel Laureate Shockley calls "speeding up the hunch mechanism" by connecting things in many new ways....

"That should solve your problem of
holding their attention, Miss Hobbs."

The Saturday Evening Post
© The Curtis Publishing Company

CHAPTER SIX

Completing the Creative Process — From Ideas to Action!

Although we may see the infinite potential for spinning our mental kaleidoscopes, forming unlimited new associations or ideas, we are often unable to generate needed ideas on demand. We then turn to "incubation."

Incubation refers to that period in the creative process when we are not involved in conscious activity with respect to our problem. Often, during or after such a period, insights or ideas seemingly emerge from within us magically.

A pertinent example involved a little girl who had been trying unsuccessfully for several days to reinsert a rope-belt into her pajama bottom. One afternoon, while rushing in from play to get an ice cube from the freezer, the idea suddenly occurred to her that she could wet and "freeze" the rope into a circle or horseshoe. Then she could easily slide it through the opening in her pajamas.

Countless anecdotes in the literature recount instances of breakthroughs in difficult problems when a person is detached from conscious attention to the problem. In fact, until the 1950s, the literature on creativity often suggested that incubation was the only way to generate creative solutions to problems. What we had to do was soak up data conscientiously and vigorously, and then simply wait for the ideas to miraculously occur between periods of deliberate effort.

But more recent findings in the study of creativity indicate that we don't always have to sit and wait for ideas to occur — as you may have seen for yourself in the previous chapter. Methods like those we have been practicing are designed to re-tap the flow of ideas when they seem to dry up. But, we can also turn to incubation....

110

"If the answer should happen to come to me after school hours, I'll phone you."

Reprinted by permission of the Chicago Tribune-New York News Syndicate, Inc.

By detaching ourselves during incubation we have deferred judgment or closure on the problem. As the problem "simmers" in the back of the mind or "on our back-burner," we attend to other things or problems and allow our senses full play upon our broader environment.

With respect to consideration of the problem, it might be reasonable to suppose that we are in a sort of hypnotic state; that is, we have given ourselves the suggestion to work on the problem and have then put it out of our consciousness. Input from our environment bombards the fringes of the problem until suddenly one element (such as the ice cube for the little girl) connects with an element of the problem and triggers it up into momentary awareness. This may occur in much the same way as a remote association is suddenly formed when we consciously attempt to produce ideas under deferred judgment. But note that the idea would not occur if the elements needed for the connection (beyond those observed during the incubative moment) were not implanted in the mind prior to incubation. Without the requisite links in our minds, we could be bombarded with apples while resting under a tree yet never come up with the law of gravity. We can dramatize this by pointing out that poems in Chinese do not occur to English poets.

Have We Overlooked Linkages?

Incubation enables the mind to attend to items of our past experience while we focus consciously upon other items in our present awareness. Links may be formed which are often overlooked when we search consciously for relationships. The conscious mind is limited in the number of ideas it can attend to at one time. Subconsciously, however, the mind is capable of much additional activity.

Let me demonstrate the way incubation works by using an analogy. Focus your eyes on an object. Now move your eyes a short distance and focus on another object near the first one. Can you still see the first object "in the corner of your eye?" This may illustrate how a problem remains "in the back of your mind," your subconscious mind. In this state, data that you might not combine intentionally becomes intermingled until an unusual combination or idea occurs. It may happen while you are involved in some other activity or even during sleep or rest....

112

"I hate to wake him — he might be in the middle of something big."

When was the last time you tried the old trick of rubbing your stomach in a circular motion while patting your head simultaneously with the other hand? If you consciously start both operations at the same time, you may find it difficult or even impossible. However, if you begin one operation, continue it until it does not require conscious thought, and then start the other, you can usually handle the two operations easily. In effect, the first movement has been pushed into the subconscious, while the second operation is consciously being attended to. Incubation seems to work in a similar way.

The idea suddenly emerging from incubation will often be embryonic and fragmentary, sometimes quite strange. It seldom seems to be the complete answer to the problem.

For example, a physician was frustrated by the hazy information that patients gave about their condition when phoning during an emergency. One day, he suddenly visualized a heart patient calling him on the phone. When the patient tried to describe the strange rhythm of his heartbeat, the doctor commanded him to place the mouthpiece to his chest. The daydreaming doctor then imagined he heard the heartbeat. Snapping out of his reverie, he phoned a colleague and asked him to hold the mouthpiece to his chest. The doctor was disappointed not to hear a heartbeat.

The idea became a reality years later, however, after intensive study and development involving electronic engineers, among others. A special instrument was finally devised to enable a doctor to listen to the heartbeat over the phone. Thus the conception of a new idea may be exciting, but its development and birth into a valuable product is usually quite painful.

Did You Write It Down?

A new idea may disappear just as quickly and mysteriously as it appeared. Did you ever think of an idea during a conversation and lose it before being able to communicate it? Or have you awakened with a solution, smiled with satisfaction, fallen back to sleep relieved, and later awoke but were unable to recall the solution? Because ideas frequently disappear, it is important to cultivate the habit of recording them immediately after they occur instead of trusting them to memory. Some people carry 3x5 cards or scraps of paper for that purpose. A dusty dashboard on a car can serve as a "dust-board" for recording unexpected ideas. A ballpoint pen can even record notes on the skin of your hand!....

*"Couldn't you just keep a pencil and paper beside your bed for
when you have one of your little night thoughts?"*

Drawing by Stan Hunt; © 1971 The New Yorker Magazine, Inc.

When Do We Stop Deferring and Begin Judging?

When viewing a problematic situation there is no end to the number of alternatives that could be generated by using the methods discussed in this book. Obviously, this alternative-searching could be carried to a ridiculous extreme, depending on the circumstances. This chart portrays what probably occurs in creative action.

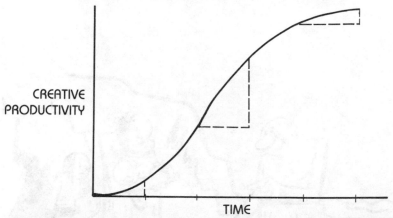

In early and late intervals of time spent, relatively little productive gain is noted. The low end of the curve might be called "complacency" — willingness to accept common associations and habit-bound solutions.

Self-satisfaction often keeps us at the low end of the curve and prevents us from reaching out with our creative talents. If we tend to become smug about what we do, we lose sight of the improvements that could be made. I am intrigued by this anonymous quotation:

If your own performance of a job looks perfect to you, it is not because you have done a perfect job, but simply because you have imperfect standards.

The upper end of the charted curve might be called "perfectionism," unwillingness to let go of an idea because it is not flawless. But perfection is only a nonattainable ideal; the best of anything is yet to be done.

So willingness to operate in the middle portion of the curve represents a happy compromise between staying "too tight" or being "too loose." It probably represents the area of maximum creative accomplishment. As Alex Osborn put it, "A fair idea put to use is better than a good idea kept forever on the polishing wheel!"....

116

"See—it ROLLS! I told you I'd figure out something
to amuse the children."

At some point toward the middle of the curve, we might well stop producing ideas and begin to evaluate them. During the evaluation (or solution-finding) phase we need to establish criteria — ways of judging — which serve as yardsticks to objectively measure the value of our ideas — how good or bad they are.

For example, if we are concerned with how long our ideas will take to implement, then we will select time as a criterion for evaluating each idea. If we are concerned with the amount of money required to implement, then cost becomes another criterion. Other possible criteria might be effect on others as well as effect on ourselves.

Just as we defer judgment in order to generate more and better ideas, it is likewise helpful to defer judgment as we think up more and better criteria beyond the obvious ones.

Try listing numerous criteria for evaluating those ideas that you generated on page 83 or 89. Look at them from many different viewpoints; defer judgment while listing as many diverse criteria as you can bring into awareness.

Criteria:

Although your own criteria are likely to be more pertinent and specific, the following checklist of general criteria might help to trigger specific ones with respect to any particular problem that you happen to be pursuing: (1) effect on objective...(2) individuals and/or groups affected...(3) costs involved...(4) moral and/or legal implications...(5) tangibles involved (materials, equipment, space, etc.)...(6) intangibles involved (opinions, attitudes, feelings, aesthetic values, etc.)...(7) new problems caused...(8) difficulties of implementation and follow-up...(9) repercussions of failure... (10) timeliness...(11) fringe benefits...(12) ease of testing and taking first steps...(13) others you now think of....

118

THE FAMILY CIRCUS   By Bil Keane

7-6

1974, The Register
and Tribune Syndicate

"Mommy! Kittycat caught a bird and brought it
home to show us! Is she good or bad?"

The Family Circus by Bil Keane. Reprinted Courtesy The Register and Tribune
Syndicate, Inc.

By deferring judgment while we list many different criteria, we develop a better sensitivity to the possible effects of the ideas we are evaluating. If we consider all conceivable effects or repercussions of a new product or idea before we put it to use, we are less likely to find out later that there is something wrong with it. Even though you cannot go on listing criteria forever, any more than you can go on listing ideas forever, most people make the mistake of considering too few criteria rather than too many.

Can We Pretest Our Ideas Mentally?

The development of sufficient criteria enhances our sensitivity to new challenges or problems that might result from the implementation of new ideas. Criteria can help us recognize and appreciate shortcomings, deficiencies and loopholes. Sufficient criteria can help us prejudge whether ideas will work successfully in dealing with the problem.

By way of analogy, suppose we were building a worktable and we were seeking an appropriate piece of lumber for the top. If we had a large pile from which to choose, we would have certain considerations or "yardsticks" in mind as we looked through the selection — length, width, thickness, hardness, freedom from knots, freedom from warp, etc. Similarly, we must have certain considerations or criteria in mind if we are to do an effective job of selecting the most appropriate idea from among a whole "pile" of ideas on hand.

Since some criteria assume more importance than others, it may be advisable to group criteria in the order of their relative importance. Then we may even decide that while meeting some criteria is merely desirable, meeting other criteria is not only desirable but essential....

THE FAMILY CIRCUS   By Bil Keane

"Mommy, is playing 'beach' in the kitty litter
a no-no?"

The Family Circus by Bil Keane. Reprinted Courtesy The Register and Tribune
Syndicate, Inc.

Oftentimes it would be appropriate to modify or refine our ideas before evaluating them against our criteria. The original ideas might be likened to raw materials, out of which we can form and polish solutions, and ultimately plans for action.

Originality in ideas is a necessary but insufficient condition for creativity. For example, if I were stretching for new uses for a coat hanger, an original or remote thought of using it as a ring for Saturn might surface. Refining this original thought might lead to the notion of making a ring-toss game.

It probably wouldn't serve much useful purpose to evaluate "ring for Saturn," an off-beat idea that emerged via deferred judgment, against criteria set for uses for a coat hanger. However, by adapting or refining the original idea, the ring-toss game might be judged seriously against the criteria.

Use the grid pictured below, or your own adaptation. Under the IDEAS column, enter a few that you like best from pages 83 and 89. Under CRITERIA place several that you consider most important from page 117. Rate all ideas under each criterion heading as either Excellent, Good, Fair, Poor, etc., until all blocks are filled. Choose the idea, combination or adptation that now looks most promising to you, and devise a plan for putting it into effect. Incidentally, you might adapt a poorly rated one by changing it to meet the criteria on which it failed. More on that in Part II.

Deferred judgment often leads to strange but intriguing ideas which can then be put into realistic perspective. Some of these ideas can be adapted into workable and acceptable solutions which are better than anything else we have. But occasionally the most prosaic idea still turns out best....

Reprinted by permission of the Chicago Tribune-New York News Syndicate, Inc.

Summary

We have discussed sensing and defining problems, generating ideas, and then evaluating the ideas by applying criteria. Having carefully selected the most promising of our ideas, we might be tempted to feel that we have reached the pinnacle of success, that we have solved our problem. But rarely is this so; for implementing a solution-idea almost always presents a new challenge of making our chosen idea acceptable.

The new "implementation-challenge" presents a continuing exercise in creative problem-solving, just as the case of our original problem for which we sought fresh ideas. It involves preparing our solution-idea for any problems that might arise during its application.

Although implementation frequently requires more creative effort than originating the idea, it does culminate in creative action and achievement, our ultimate goal. More opportunities to experience this will be provided in the next section as we apply the basic alternating process of defer judgment, diverge, FLOW and stop temporarily, converge, DECIDE within each phase of a five-step creative problem-solving process:

- Fact-Finding
- Problem-Finding
- Idea-Finding
- Solution-Finding (involving criteria-listing)
- Acceptance-Finding (or Implementation)

The problem-solving process outlined above may appear to be similar, in terms of its steps or logical processes, to those formulated by John Dewey, Graham Wallace and others. However, the plus ingredient introduced is the deliberate and exaggerated use of the imagination, a powerful force when effectively harnessed within a total problem-solving model.

The five steps are merely a guide rather than a strict formula for problem solving. Frequently a change of sequence may be introduced into the process; and it is always advisable to provide plenty of opportunity for incubation. The main emphasis throughout each step is to accumulate alternatives before zeroing in on the better ones. And remember that nothing is final, for every solution presents many new challenges....

124

Intellectualizing the creative problem-solving processes is different from internalizing them effectively — just as attending a lecture on physical education is different from attending a program for physical education.

How's Your Attitude?

On the final day of one of our Creative Problem-Solving Institutes, a company executive remarked, "If you could only have gotten us into this frame of mind on the first day, we could have accomplished so much more!" I explained that a major objective of the Institute was to develop just such attitudes as he was now experiencing. I also explained that we had talked about attitudes in our orientation session, but then proceeded to provide experiences that developed the desired frame of mind in the participants. Simply talking about it at the beginning of the Institute hadn't produced the desired change.

"Aha," exclaimed the executive, "I see now, that you have certainly accomplished your objective." He realized that he was then ready to take advantage of the new viewpoints and attitudes in facing his company's problems.

How Important Is Practice?

You may have to practice using the creative problem-solving procedures for some time before you become comfortable and productive with them. I question whether a person can fully understand or fully appreciate the meaning of concepts like deferred judgment until he/she has experientially internalized them. Part II will help you do just that....

CHAPTER SEVEN

Introduction to Part II:
Warming Up to the Full Process

This part guides you through a number of creative problem-solving experiences involving challenges or problems that you set for yourself in each chapter. In each case, stretch for maximum sensitivity to the challenges, opportunities or problems in your life. You may discover many opportunities to explore that you hadn't thought of before.

Each succeeding chapter provides you with fewer and fewer cues to trigger your imagination and to guide you through the alternating process of "flowing" and then "deciding" at each of the steps. If you find that the cues are more than you need for the desired flow and resulting ahas, then progress at your own pace or move ahead to the next chapter, where less cues are given.

Unless you are truly distracted from your flow by the cueing, I urge you to go through all of the chapters so that you may pick up some fine points as well as experience more and more stretching. This groundwork should help you to feel more comfortable and effective when you "go it alone" in Chapters 11 and 12.

Are You Willing to Stretch Your Mental Muscles?

Each step of the process gives you another opportunity to achieve some new and relevant associations — ahas — the heart of the creative process. If you skip a step, you can still reach a solution, but it is less likely to be a good, workable one. Likewise if you don't stretch for many alternatives in each step, you can still find your solution — but it may not be as effective as if you thought up a greater amount of alternatives from which to choose. There is no guarantee that following a step, or stretching within it, will produce an important aha; however, extensive research and practice has consistently demonstrated the probability that you will find more and better ahas, resulting in better solutions or decisions. You will be less apt to be confronted with superficial solutions or those that deal with symptoms rather than underlying causes....

ANDY CAPP by Reggie Smythe, Copyright Daily Mirror Newspapers Ltd. Dist. Field
Newspaper Syndicate.

Perhaps you can experience what I'm talking about rather quickly and simply by trying the following experiment:

- List a challenge or problem you have...

- Now jot down your first reaction as to what you should do about it...

Did you have an aha? If you did, be grateful! It's like hitting the jackpot with one try. But chances are that you didn't, since ahas rarely are that simple.

- Now, jot down something you know — are aware of — about the challenge or problem...

- Next, define the problem as you see it...

- Now, state your way of solving it...

- Next, state your reason for deciding on that way...

- Finally, note how you will put your solution into effect....

Broadsides

Any ahas that time? It could have happened as you, in a sense, went through the five steps very quickly, reacting to your first thought in each step. But it's not very likely.

Now try breaking past the immediate connection you made at each step by adding three or four more thoughts — different alternatives — under each step; defer judgment as you allow several alternatives to flow freely in each step.

- Fact-finding (what you know about it):

- Problem-finding (different ways of viewing or defining the problem): Try to start each definition with the words, "In what ways might I....":

- Idea-finding (ideas that might help solve it):

- Solution-finding (criteria for evaluating the ideas — means for judging — reasons the ideas are good or bad):

- Acceptance-finding (ways to get my best idea(s) into effect):

- Plan of Action (choose the best way(s) to get your selected idea(s) into effect; add a timetable for carrying out your plan):

The Lumpits

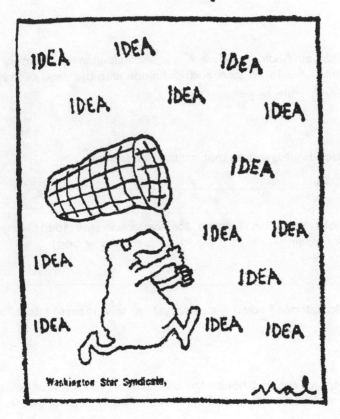

Cartoon by Malcolm Hancock.

Let's hope that you caught a worthwhile idea that time, and came up with a new and relevant plan of action. If you didn't, some of the experiences that follow will help to increase the probability that it will happen the next time.

Before we begin our full stretch in the next chapter, try one more quick creative problem-solving run-through. This time we will emphasize "right-brain" focus — imagery — almost totally. In all subsequent chapters, we will combine the verbal and the imagery constantly as we stretch and flow through the process.

Have You Tried Relaxation?

Choose a challenge or concern from your list on page 23. Then take a moment to relax yourself fully from head to foot. Try to tighten each muscle as totally as possible, then let go so that you can experience release of the tension in each individual muscle. Check once more for any remaining tension. If you find any, concentrate on that spot by tensing the muscle even more and then letting go.

Now, in a more relaxed state, proceed to image as follows, making notations or sketches when significant thoughts occur.

- **Fact-Finding:** Visualize the situation or challenge you have chosen. "See" in your imagination everything you know about it. Watch what is happening...who or what is involved...when, where, how and why it is happening. Let the pictures flow through your mind as in a dream...

- **Problem-Finding:** Now fantasize or "daydream" a scenario as to how you would like the situation to look. What would your wish be about the situation if you could wave a magic wand and alter it any way you'd like? Imagine it that way...

- **Idea-Finding:** Begin changing some of the details in the picture of the situation as it presently exists to make it more like what your fantasy-wish portrayed. Change the original picture bit-by-bit. Magnify, minify or rearrange parts, or all of it, in ways that bring it more and more toward your ideal fantasy. (You might like to do this by visualizing your fantasized scenario on one TV screen and the situation as it presently exists on a second screen. Then start modifying the present picture as explained.) Don't be intimidated by any past conditioning that you may have experienced about fantasizing, daydreaming, wishing, etc....

THE LOCKHORNS

"WIPE THAT WISH OFF YOUR FACE!"

Now focus on the changes you seem to like most.

- **Solution-Finding:** Picture and feel how you might react to the kinds of changes you selected, as well as how others might feel or react. "Jump into their skins" and picture your selected changes from their points of view, from as many viewpoints as possible...

- **Acceptance-Finding:** Keeping those multiple feelings and reactions in mind, begin picturing some of the modifications that might make your fantasy more workable or acceptable to yourself and others. Piece together the best image of yourself dealing effectively with the original challenge or concern. Try for as much detail as you can...

Then make notes of the best action plan that you have now created, including a timetable for carrying out the plan....

My Plan:

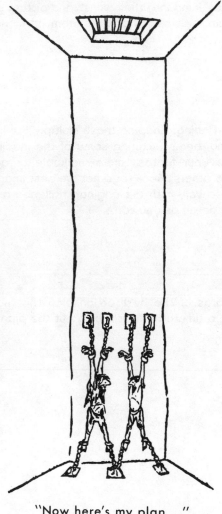

"Now here's my plan..."

With a bit of stretch, you may have had an aha, even if only a five- or ten-volt one, that may have led to a worthwhile plan for dealing with at least a small part of the challenge. If you didn't, the extensive stretch called for in the next chapter is almost bound to generate a few ahas on your next problem-choice.

Can We Habitually Break Habits?

Psychologists sometimes raise the question of whether learning specific methods of solving problems may create "sets" or fixed habits that interfere with a way of solving a particular problem. It is precisely against any such rigidity — such interference with flexible associations — that this book is designed. In a sense, it attempts to establish habits against habits (a set against set) when approaching new situations, yet ones which allow a person to live, in full awareness, with certain temporary sets or habits required in our society.

Instead of merely reacting in a habitual way to your awareness as you may have done at the top of page 129, you can learn to:

- re-examine the situation for more facts;
- re-define the problem (it probably isn't the same as you first thought);
- generate alternative ideas as reactions or responses to the problem as now viewed;
- become aware of the multiple repercussions or consequences associated with the ideas being considered; and
- develop the best idea as fully as possible before putting it to use.

In the next chapter you may be doing this in an exaggerated way, but by Chapter 11 it should become natural to you. Hopefully, you will make it a habit to automatically break habit in forming mental associations, so that you may see new and relevant opportunities, solutions and decisions....

"Remember, son, if at first you don't succeed, re-evaluate the situation, draw up various hypotheses for your failure, choose reasonable corrective measures, and try, try again."

Reprinted by permission of Randy Glasbergen.

CHAPTER EIGHT

How About a S T R E T C H
Through the Process?

This chapter will provide you with an opportunity to stretch your creative processes in many diverse ways in sensing and solving your
problems. You will expand greatly on what you did in the previous
chapter as you take charge. I will merely offer stimuli that may increase the probability of your deriving some ahas. These ahas should
serve to reinforce you in modifying your thinking-behavior to include
more and more of the emphases suggested.

The deliberate development of creative behavior might be
viewed as an exaggerated push for change. We assume that the
imagination regresses, when it is not prodded, to more natural and
desirable levels that contain a reasonable balance between imagination and judgment. Stretching beyond the normal limits of our
imagination serves to "overcorrect" much in the same way as we
would in attempting to straighten a bent tree.

The experience that follows will serve as an example of one of
the infinite number of "compositions" that might be conceived by
putting the pieces of the process together in a variety of arrange-
ments, just as an infinite number of musical compositions can be
generated by rearranging the notes within various theoretical
frameworks.

As I provide the stimuli for your thoughts, allow them to flow freely
without analyzing or evaluating them in any way. Don't let anything
inhibit your thoughts....

140

Allow yourself at least an hour-and-a-half to two hours on this chapter. If you are pressed for time, plan an incubation break and finish it at a later time. You will be working on something important to you so you should allow yourself all the time you need.

If you should happen to solve a problem to your satisfaction early in the process, proceed to another challenge. Should you find that you are accomplishing something important and my stimuli are interfering with it, leave the book and work ahead however you like while you are flowing productively. Check back later to see what special techniques I added, and use them on another challenge if you wish.

What is Our Objective?

Remember that the objective is to accomplish something valuable to you. My diverse stimuli are designed to increase that likelihood. Do not read ahead before responding to each instruction, unless you are only interested in understanding what I am doing rather than experiencing your creative processes. If you should decide to read only and not to record as suggested, I urge you to at least think your responses to each instruction before reading on.

Please don't try to figure out the rationale for the particular stimuli I chose; each is merely a way of potentially tapping new flow, new associations. Just respond spontaneously, and then go back later and analyze if you wish.

Be aware that this exercise is often given at the completion of a creative-studies course or Creative Problem-Solving Institute after intensive practice in processes designed to increase the flow of ideas. So, speed is not important right now. Just move along from item to item, trying always to allow your thoughts to flow wherever they take you in response to my stimuli. And if something is not clear to you, make whatever sense of it you can at that moment and respond to that without further worry. Good luck in your adventure!

Now, let's sensitize ourselves to challenges in our lives....

142

DISCOVERING CHALLENGES:

1. List, sketch or symbolize any challenges you have in any aspect of your life...

2. Jot down additional thoughts as they are triggered by the following questions...

   What would you like to do, have, accomplish?
   What idea would you like to get working?
   What do you wish would happen?
   What relationship would you like to improve?
   What would you like to do better?
   What do you wish you had more time for?
   What do you wish you had more money for?
   What more would you like to get out of life?
   What are your unfulfilled goals?
   What turns you on?
   What angered you recently?
   What makes you tense, anxious?
   What misunderstandings did you have?
   What have you complained about?
   With whom would you like to get along better?
   What changes for the worse do you sense in attitudes of others?
   What would you like to get others to do?
   What changes will you have to introduce?
   What takes too long?
   What is wasted?
   What is too complicated?
   What "bottlenecks" exist?
   In what ways are you inefficient?
   What wears you out?
   What turns you off?
   What would you like to organize better?

Used by permission of United Feature Syndicate, Inc.

3. List at least six roles that you play in your life (example: daughter, politician, student, etc.)...

4. Now imagine yourself in each role and make notes of any more challenges that come to mind...

5. Think of a nonverbal message that you could give to someone you know. Imagine how you might feel doing it. Then add more challenges to your list...

6. Choose (from page 143 and above) one challenge, concern or idea that you would most like to start doing something about....

WOODY ALLEN

Reprinted by permission of King Features Syndicate, Inc.

FACT-FINDING:

1. List, sketch or symbolize what you know about the concern, challenge or idea chosen...

2. Let the following questions trigger more data about the situation...

   What is or is not happening?

   Who is or is not concerned?

   When does or doesn't this occur?

   Where does or doesn't this occur?

   Why does or doesn't it happen?

   How does or doesn't it happen?

3. Make sure you've noted how you and others do and do not feel about the situation. This is an important part of the data. Try to understand, not necessarily agree. Defer judgment as you record all the feelings you are aware of....

THE FAMILY CIRCUS   By Bil Keane

1974, The Register
and Tribune Syndicate

"I could stay as clean as you do if I wasn't down here so close to the ground."

The Family Circus by Bil Keane. Reprinted Courtesy The Register and Tribune Syndicate, Inc.

4. Smell deeply a variety of odors emitted from foliage, spices, perfumes, ashes or other items from the immediate environment. Deal with each slowly, reflecting, ruminating as you breathe in each aroma. Record any thoughts or memories that the fragrances "trigger"...

   NOTE: The sense of smell is one of the most powerful triggers for awakening memories. Remember to rely on it anytime you are trying to stimulate diverse associations.

5. Connect to your earlier facts whatever you can from the thoughts you just recorded...

6. Make note of your strengths, modesty aside. Brag about your personality, your abilities, etc. Think of any compliment or appraisal anyone ever gave you. Look for elements of strength that they stated or implied...

7. Now add new thoughts that may surface as you contemplate those strengths. These thoughts and feelings can be considered part of your data....

PEANUTS

I'VE COME TO THE CONCLUSION THAT YOU'RE A VERY FRIENDLY FELLOW, CHARLIE BROWN

WELL, THANK YOU, PATTY...I APPRECIATE THE COMPLIMENT

DON'T MENTION IT...I THINK THAT'S THE LEAST A PERSON CAN SAY ABOUT YOU...

SOMEDAY I'D LIKE TO HEAR MORE THAN JUST THE **LEAST**!

8. Don't hesitate to add the most as you think of any further strengths and their implications...

9. Experience your immediate environment through your senses: look, listen, taste, touch, smell. Then add any thoughts that surface from your memory bank — facts that may be relevant but were forgotten...
   NOTE: Our mind has a remarkable capacity to store data as compared with its relative inability under normal conditions to retrieve that information. We have much more information than we realize, if only we can "shake it loose."

10. Try imaging the challenge, concern or idea that you have been describing. Close your eyes and imagine it as fully as you can. "See" it, "feel" it, "hear" it, "taste" it, "smell" it. Use your imagination to note details as fully and as vividly as you can....

THE FAMILY CIRCUS   By Bil Keane

"I was just dreaming — y'know, when you close your eyes and the picture comes on?"

The Family Circus by Bil Keane. Reprinted Courtesy The Register and Tribune Syndicate, Inc.

PROBLEM-FINDING:

1. Flow with as many questions as possible surrounding the situation that you described. Try to start the questions with the words, "In what ways might I...?" "What might I do to...?" "How might I...?" If "Should I" questions come to mind, change them to "In what ways might I decide...?" If questions calling for more facts occur, word them as "In what ways might I find out...?" Let your thoughts flow without analyzing or judging the appropriateness of each problem-statement you list...

2. Now think of a "peak" joyous experience in your life. Close your eyes and relive that experience in your imagination. Daydream it...

3. List additional "In what ways might I...?" statements of your problem as a result of connections you might make with the peak experience you imaged...

4. Stop a moment and ask, "What is the real problem? The essence of it? "What is my basic objective?" "What do I want to accomplish here?" Ask "Why" of each question you have listed: "Why do I want to do this?" Then answer, "In order to...." As a result of these questions and answers, try to restate and broaden your problem. For example, if you asked "Why" of the problem, "How might I catch the mouse?", it might lead to the answer, "In order to get rid of it." This leads to the restatement, "How might I get rid of the mouse?" The latter allows for more possibilities. List several restatements of your problem....

We'll probably fall between "In what ways might we turn off the faucets," and "In what ways might we filter the water for swimming."

Reprinted by permission of Timi Gleason.

5. Draw a personal symbol to represent yourself...

6. Now write additional "In what ways might I...?" questions connecting interpretations or feelings about the symbol to the situation you are defining....

7. You start out in any perplexing situation with a "mess." You find the "fuzzy" challenge within the "mess" and then you state the challenge as broadly as possible, as on page 153. The broad problem then breaks down into a number of subproblems. Break down your earlier questions into aspects, parts, stages, operations, etc. List more "In what ways might I...?" questions that get at specific aspects of the problem — such as "In what ways might I use available resources more fully?"....

THE FAMILY CIRCUS   By Bil Keane

The Family Circus by Bil Keane. Reprinted Courtesy The Register and Tribune Syndicate, Inc.

8. Try once more to imagine the details of the challenge, problem or idea you are working on. Close your eyes and see how many facts or data you can picture in your imagination...

9. What do you wish would happen concerning the observations that you made when using your imagination? List as many wishes as you like, with no restraints or judgment...

10. Convert each wish into additional "In what ways might I...?" problem-statements. For example, if you wished that the budget hadn't been cut, you might list, "In what ways might I accomplish objectives with limited funding?" "In what ways might I recoup funds by cutting waste?", etc. If you wished that you were younger, you might record, "In what ways might I regain my youthful outlook?", "In what ways might I look younger?", etc. Try seeing it in several new ways....

Reprinted by permission of King Features Syndicate, Inc.

11. From among all of those that you have listed, select the "In what ways might I...?" question which looks most promising or interesting to work on first. Try to make the best choice for now — a starting point for your idea-finding efforts at this moment in time. Save the other problem-statements that look promising or important to you for another time...

  NOTE: Even now the other statements are likely to work subconsciously to trigger related ideas, since you have "loaded your computer" with these diverse ways of viewing the problem.

IDEA-FINDING:

1. Deferring judgment as fully as you can and allowing your ideas to flow freely, list, sketch or symbolize as many ideas as possible for attacking the problem you just chose...

2. Magnify, minify, rearrange, etc., in seeking additional ideas. Ask yourself what would happen if you made something bigger, smaller, reversed elements or positions, etc. Visualize each of these changes. As you imagine them, do not evaluate the ideas that occur; just continue to jot them down....

The Saturday Evening Post
© 1965 The Curtis Publishing Company

"I just hope it isn't a contact lens."

3. In searching for additional ideas, look for strange analogies to the situation that you are working on. For example, if the situation has to do with the office or home, think of a "circus" or a "space-ship" and draw relationships from these other settings...

4. Listen to music with a "descriptive" quality that will tend to stir some response from you. Hum or sing it if none is available to you now. Concentrate on the music and forget about what you have been writing; "incubate" momentarily on the problem. Try moving physically with the music in some new way. Make new "physical connections," if only with your head, fingers, toes, etc...

5. As the music concludes, write or sketch more ideas that come to mind. See if your body movement suggested anything, even symbolically...

6. Close your eyes, and imagine yourself in your own "personal paradise." Then write or sketch more ideas, connecting aspects of your personal paradise with the problem that you are working on....

NATIONAL ENQUIRER

By permission of the National Enquirer and Mel Yauk.

7. Take other imaginary trips (or actual ones, if time is unlimited) through your favorite department store, museum, zoo, etc., and connect aspects with the problem at hand...

8. Try to "force" relationships with what you see, feel, hear, smell, taste in your present environment, triggering and noting additional ideas...

9. Looking back at some of the ideas that seem interesting, imagine each one as though it existed, as though it were actually taking place. Try to magnify, minify and rearrange each idea in your imagination in as many ways as possible, deferring judgment and jotting down modifications or new ideas that emerge...

   NOTE: You are still attempting to add to your total idea-finding list, out of which you will then select ones to evaluate and develop. So, don't hesitate to continue jotting down strange or wild ideas.

10. Choose from your total list the idea(s) or combinations that look most promising or interesting and/or that you like best at this time. The choice may be totally "gut-level," even if you have no awareness of how your selection can be implemented....

    NOTE: If your original problem-statement was quite broad, you may find that many of your ideas are really "subproblems." For example, consider the problem "In what ways might I become more effective in my job?" You might respond with, "learn more about the entire organization and how it interrelates," "develop my professional skills," etc. These, in turn, would become "specific approaches" — subproblems — for further probing ("In what ways might I learn more about the entire organization and how it interrelates?" "In what ways might I develop my professional skills?") before continuing on to solution-finding.

164

SOLUTION-FINDING:

1. List, sketch or symbolize evaluative criteria to assist you in judging how "good" or "bad" the chosen ideas are. Consider who or what might be effected, elements that might make it fail, or those that might make it better...

2. In your imagination, be something in the situation other than yourself. Become another person, an animal or a thing, imagining how the ideas look from that point of view. Then add additional criteria from the new connections that you make...

3. List as many "Will it...?" questions as you can. "Will it cost too much?" "Will it adversely effect someone?" Etc....

Reprinted by permission of King Features Syndicate, Inc.

4. Visualize others reacting as you tell them about your ideas. See their expressions, their "nonverbals." Then add any further criteria that you become aware of...

5. Review all the criteria that you have recorded. Choose those you feel are most important, adding any you wish from the checklist of general criteria on page 117...

6. Set up a grid to evaluate all the ideas that you are considering against each criterion that you selected. Get a more objective picture of each idea's potential. Use any rating system you like: letters, numbers, or even smiles or frowns in each rating box....

> NOTE: if you should discover now or during Acceptance-finding that your favorite idea has some shortcomings that you hadn't been aware of, that can be an important aha too. We might call that a negative aha.

"What's the opposite of 'Eureka!'?"

Drawing by Dana Fradon; © 1975 The New Yorker Magazine, Inc.

ACCEPTANCE-FINDING:

1. Work now with the idea you would most like to use first. If it doesn't generally meet the criteria, "tailor" it to fit them. Fantasize it working, then adapt the fantasy to reality by modifying it as necessary. Use the criteria as "tools" to work your raw ideas into usable ones. For example, if "money" is an important criterion on which the idea rates poorly, record ideas under such new questions as "In what ways might I reduce the cost of this?" "In what ways might I find more money for this?" Defer judgment, recording all ideas that occur...

2. Defer judgment and produce a free flow of suggestions for gaining acceptance and putting your idea to use — suggestions that aid in implementing, insuring success, improving the original idea, showing its advantages, gaining enthusiasm of yourself or others, overcoming objections, anticipating possible misconceptions, pretesting, etc....

3. Close your eyes. Concentrate on physically relaxing yourself from the top of your head to the tips of your toes, thus providing another moment of "incubation." As you discover points of tension, try tensing the muscle even more; then relax it fully....

STRICTLY BUSINESS   by McFeatters

SUGGESTIONS

PRACTICAL

IMPRACTICAL

STUPID

Dale McFeatters

"We welcome all kinds of suggestions."

4. Close your eyes again. Visualize modifications as you adapt your idea to suit all those concerned. In your mind, notice your reactions and expressions, as well as those of others. Keep on adapting the idea until everyone seems to feel good about it — until both you and the others smile happily...

5. Record the adaptations you made...

6. List additional ways of getting your idea to work. Emphasize specifics, particularly those which are verifiable or demonstrable. For example, change "cut down on smoking," to "smoke one cigarette less each succeeding day until I've stopped entirely." Apply the checklist, "Who, what, when, where, why, how": Who might help? What other people and groups? What resources might I use? What special times, occasions or places? Why might they want to do it? How might I get their cooperation?, etc. Defer judgment as you flow freely with your ideas...

7. Think of your favorite food, sport or hobby. Try to relate something from any one of these to the idea you want to get working effectively. Defer judgment as you jot down associations...

8. Choose ideas you can use from the entire Acceptance-finding list even if they deal with only one small part of the problem or challenge....

172

9. **Now spell out** in detail a **plan** for the moment. **List as many** specifics **as possible, including first steps you will take, schedule of follow-ups, etc. What will be your one push up?** Be sure to include something that you will do physically before tomorrow night that will commit you to action. It might be an initial phone call, contact, letter, purchase, movement, etc. Also schedule among your next steps a time when you will come back to other problem-statements or ideas you recorded in this chapter...

10. Close your eyes. Relax as fully as you can. Imagine yourself lying comfortably in a lounge chair, a hammock, a haystack, a rowboat or the like. Before you is a large TV set which you can manipulate from a remote control in your hand. Turn on the TV and see yourself putting your plan into action just as you would like to see it happen. See every detail, every expression and reaction, yours as well as those of others involved...

11. Now bring into the "picture" an unexpected development. Using your imagination, "watch" the consequences...

12. Add further adaptations to your recorded plan, taking into account what you just "saw" so as to further insure the effectiveness of your plan...

13. Visualize and record new challenges that might result from implementing the plan....

174

BROTHER JUNIPER

"For a while there I didn't think you were going to make it."

BROTHER JUNIPER by Fred McCarthy. Copyright Field Enterprises, Inc. Courtesy of Field Newspaper Syndicate.

14. As a final step, make any modifications desirable as a result of the new challenges you just listed. We nearly always find that before solution-ideas can be utilized or implemented, they need to undergo some changes in order to fit our needs precisely; that is, in order to cope with challenges that might arise in applying the ideas...

   NOTE: This process resembles the one used in the clothing business. A garment progresses from the drawing board and fabric to the model, then to the purchaser, after which it must be tailored to the customer's dimensions. Likewise, we tailor an idea carefully before applying it. Early tailoring of an idea may be relatively easy and inexpensive compared with later action often required to rectify a defect in an idea.

Is Your Plan Ready to Stand on Its Own?

We are like parents to our creative ideas. As with children, we want to prepare them to "weather" the needs of the practical life. Implementation involves preparing our ideas for any demands that may be made on them or from any problems that might arise in their use.

A solution or a plan of action might be likened to a landing on a stairway, a place to rest; a place to get a perspective of our position and our direction, to see where we are going and where we have come from in our thinking.

An example illustrative of how new challenges emerge from present "solutions" involves a team of electronics engineers who had the problem of designing a special-purpose camera. They created a camera that met the special needs very effectively. Since the camera was very costly and could not be used as generally as might be desired, the emerging challenge was to reduce the cost. By creatively approaching this challenge, they were able to reduce the cost drastically. This in turn created new challenges in selling the camera to broader markets. And so on. One "solution" becomes another challenge....

176

Reprinted by permission of King Features Syndicate, Inc.

How About Incubation?

I hope you gained some new insights into the concern you chose to deal with. If you didn't, then let incubation play a stronger role. Get away from it for a while and let new associations be triggered by random input from other daily activities. Keep pad and pencil handy in order to catch those fleeting thoughts that may well up into your consciousness.

Later today or tomorrow, look over what you wrote in this chapter, including the challenges associated with implementing the idea you would like to use. Also review carefully problem-statements or ideas other than the first ones you chose, to see whether new possibilities emerge. Play imaginatively with what you wrote or what you captured during incubation. See whether new directions become apparent toward a viable solution and a plan of action.

If nothing emerges, try another period of incubation. Continue alternating between deliberate involvement with the challenge and a period of conscious detachment that allows the incubation process to take over. This alternating procedure should increase the likelihood of a breakthrough or a new insight, as compared with working doggedly on the problem or relying only on the chance association during incubation.

Remember, it is a probability game that we are playing. We may not be able to guarantee ourselves an insight or solution, but we can significantly increase the probability of finding it. Repeated research and experience has borne this out.

NOTE: Each cartoon from here on is designed to stimulate your work on the subsequent page rather than to cap a point from the preceding one....

178

CHAPTER NINE

Are You Ready for Accomplishing With Less Prompters?

Wait until you are fresh and rested before beginning this second run-through of the process. Your timing can have significant bearing on your results as well as on your enjoyment of the process. The cartoons on the left-hand pages are geared for "right-brain" messages as you move on; reflect on them as you react to the copy on the pages opposite them.

This time choose another challenge, concern or idea that you would like to do something about. It could be something from the list you created on pages 143-145 of the previous chapter, or something that emerged from that entire experience.

FACT-FINDING:

1. List, sketch or symbolize facts and feelings about the situation you have chosen. See how much you can record about it in a free-flowing, deferred-judgment manner.

   What is or is not happening?

   Who is or is not concerned?

   When does or doesn't this occur?

   Where does or doesn't this occur?

   Why does or doesn't it happen?

   How does or doesn't it happen?

   Flow with these facts and feelings...

2. Try visualizing the challenge, concern or idea you have been describing. Close your eyes and imagine it as fully as you can. "See" it, "feel" it, "hear" it, "taste" it, "smell" it. Try for as clear a mental picture as you can image...

3. Add as many more details as you are now able....

THE FAMILY CIRCUS By Bil Keane

10-16
1975, The Register
and Tribune Syndicate

"Why don't eggs have a tab you can pull?"

The Family Circus by Bil Keane. Reprinted Courtesy The Register and Tribune Syndicate, Inc.

PROBLEM-FINDING:

1. Try for as many as possible of those "In what ways might I...?" problem statements. Avoid the impulse to answer the question; just defer judgment and see how many of these questions you can raise...

2. Try once more to imagine the details of the challenge, problem or idea you are working on. Close your eyes and see how much of the detail (facts or data) you can picture in your imagination. "See" it, "feel" it, "taste" it, "smell" it, "hear" it in your imagination...

3. What do you wish would happen about what you observed in your imagination? Make as many wishes as you would like, with no concern for restraints or judgment...

4. Convert each wish into "In what ways might I...?" problem-statements...

5. Select the "In what ways might I...?" question you'd like to work on first; the one that looks most promising or intriguing; the one for which you'd most like some new ideas now...

6. Try listing synonyms for the verb and other key words in the question...

> EXAMPLE: "What ways might I toast bread?" may become "What ways might I brown and dehydrate bread?" The latter statement has enabled completely new toaster designs to be conceived by spelling out the real problem of "toasting" bread. Changing the verb in a statement of a challenge can help change our mental "set" or outlook regarding the challenge.

7. Finally, choose the words that best express the problem for you and get ready for Idea-finding....

182

Reprinted by courtesy of Vision in Design.

IDEA-FINDING:

1. Defer judgment and allow your ideas to flow freely without any evaluation at the moment. List, sketch or symbolize ideas for attacking the problem you just chose. Magnify, minify and rearrange. Look for obvious analogies as well as strange ones...

2. Try a "forced" incubation break — music, relaxation or some complete change of pace — a refreshment break, exercise, jogging, dancing, etc....

3. Record any new ideas that occurred during or after incubation...

4. Look back at some of the more interesting ideas on this page. Imagine each of them as though it existed, as though it were actually taking place. Then try to magnify, minify and rearrange the idea in your imagination in as many ways as possible; defer judgment and jot down modifications or new ideas that emerge...

5. Choose from the total page the idea(s) that look most promising or interesting, and/or that you like best at this time. Remember, if your idea is very general, you may want to consider it as a "subproblem" and generate specific ideas under it before moving on to the criteria in Solution-finding....

THE FAMILY CIRCUS   By Bil Keane

"Could I have a note for the bus driver saying it's okay for me and Greg to play football on the bus?"

The Family Circus by Bil Keane. Reprinted Courtesy The Register and Tribune Syndicate, Inc.

SOLUTION-FINDING:

1. List, sketch or symbolize evaluative criteria to assist you in determining how "good" or "bad" the ideas are. Consider elements which might make them fail, or those which might make them better, and who and what might be affected, etc. Don't forget the "Will it...?" questions...

2. Visualize others reacting to you as you tell them about your ideas. See their expressions, their "nonverbals." Then add the further criteria that you become aware of...

3. Use the most important criteria as tools to help you tailor your selected "raw" idea(s) into workable ones. Apply deferred judgment and record ways to reshape the idea(s) to fit the criteria better....

   EXAMPLE: In purchasing a house, a certain couple had included the criterion, "not a corner lot." They found a house that met all their criteria except that one. So they asked themselves, "In what ways might we enjoy the corner lot?" In brainstorming for ideas, they suddenly saw a way to use bushes to provide more privacy than they had formerly enjoyed in their previous house in the middle of the block. At that point they realized that it wasn't the corner lot that was concerning them, but lack of privacy resulting from a corner lot. If the couple had posed the question, "Why are we concerned about a corner lot?" they might have answered, "Because it wouldn't afford the privacy we like." Then they could have restated their problem as, "In what ways might we enjoy privacy on a corner lot?" This might have directed their flow of ideas to the bushes faster than the original question did. It is advisable to "massage" the problem-statement a few times before seeking ideas, whether in Problem-Finding or when we see a new problem emerge in Solution-Finding, as above.

186

ACCEPTANCE-FINDING:

1. Try a few minutes of relaxation, exercise, change of pace, etc....

2. Now produce a free flow of ideas for gaining acceptance and putting your chosen idea(s) to use. List ways to implement, insure success, improve the original idea(s), show advantages, gain enthusiasm of yourself or others, overcome objections, anticipate possible misconceptions, pretest, etc....

3. Now spell out in detail a plan for the moment. List as many specifics as possible, including first steps you will take, schedule, follow-up, etc. Remember the checklist: who, what, when, where, why and how...

4. If you want to generate a great variety of possible plans, try the morphological process described in Chapter 5. Use a variety of who's, what's, when's, where's, how's and why's as the variables to be cross-related...

5. If the idea you want to use is quite difficult to implement, use the "30 Question" checklist on page 189....

30 Questions[5]

Stretch for as many ideas as possible under each question. Then select the best ideas to weave into your final plan of action. With extended effort on this, you may achieve major breakthroughs in getting your idea into action.

1. What might I do to gain acceptance?
2. What might I do to gain enthusiasm for the idea?
3. What might I do to insure effectiveness?
4. What ways might I use criteria to show advantages?
5. What other advantages might exist? How might I dramatize them?
6. What disadvantages might exist? How might I overcome them?
7. What additional resources might help (individuals, groups, money, materials, equipment, time, authority, permission, other intangibles, etc.)? How might I obtain them?
8. What new challenges might the idea suggest?
9. How might I anticipate and meet these?
10. What objections, difficulties, limitations, obstacles might exist?
11. How might I overcome them?
12. How might I improve, safeguard or fortify the idea?
13. Who might help with the idea?
14. What group might help?
15. Who might contribute special strengths or resources? How might I get them to help?
16. Who might add an unexpected element?
17. Who might gain from the idea?
18. Who might need persuasion?
19. How might I reward myself or others for helping carry it out?
20. How might I pretest my idea?
21. What first step might I take to initiate action?
22. What next steps might follow?
23. What timing might I use?
24. What schedules might I follow?
25. What follow-up might I plan to measure progress?
26. What follow-up to allow corrective measures?
27. What follow-up to deal with unexpected repercussions?
28. What special times might I use? Days? Dates?
29. What special circumstances or occasions might I use?
30. What special places or locations might help? Where else?

And...What else? When Else? Who else? How else? Why else?....

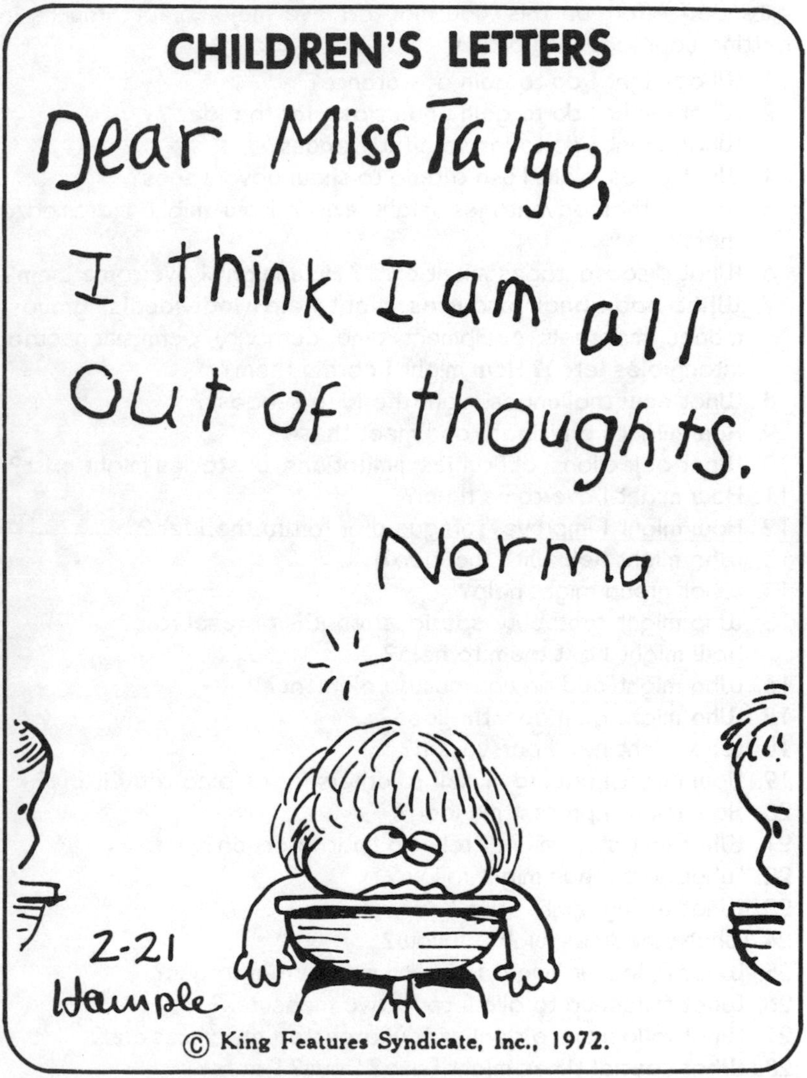

CHILDREN'S LETTERS
Dear Miss Talgo,
I think I am all
Out of thoughts.
Norma
2-21
Hample
© King Features Syndicate, Inc., 1972.

If you are all out of thoughts regarding your plan of action, then do the following...

1. Close your eyes. Relax as fully as you can. Imagine yourself lying in a very comfortable place. Before you is a large TV set. Turn on the TV and see yourself putting your plan into action just as you would like to see it happen. See every detail, every expression and reaction, yours as well as those of others involved...

2. Now bring into the "picture" an unexpected development. Using your imagination, "watch" the consequences...

3. Add more ideas to your recorded plan, taking into account what you "saw," so that you might further insure the effectiveness of your plan...

4. Imagine and list new challenges that might result from implementing the plan...

5. Review in your mind any new connections you can make as a result of the new challenges you just listed. Adapt the details of your plan accordingly. Incubate further on the plan and continue extending your effort toward meeting the challenges that you have been considering, as you put your plan into action. Remember always that "nothing is final!"...

I hope you gained some new insights this time. If you didn't, get away from your challenge for a while, incubate. Keep pad and pencil handy to capture ideas. Later on, look over all the thoughts you recorded earlier and during incubation, including other problem-statements or ideas. See whether they suggest new possibilities. Deferring judgment, force new relationships between what you already had and what materialized during incubation. If nothing emerges, try incubation again. Continue alternating between deliberate involvement and incubation. The probability of a new insight will be greater than by using either process alone. Catch those fleeting thoughts whenever they occur, not just on a "9 to 5" basis....

CHAPTER TEN

Let's Try Intensive Opportunity-Making!

Being sure that you are fresh and rested again, choose another challenge, concern or idea that you want to do something about. This time you might want to focus on a challenge that I call an "opportunity-type" (implying no urgency) rather than a "concern-type" or "obstacle-type." Some examples might be: planning new ways to use scrap materials or leftover food; a new plan for an office party; or a new way to express your love to your mate. Although you may have successfully dealt with these topics before, the process may help you to discover a whole new realm of value, enjoyment or satisfaction. Experiencing the joys of creating new and relevant plans in some of these areas will probably motivate you to apply the process in situations where nothing has to be done, where no new solutions have to be achieved. Here the process becomes great fun in and of itself, and can even provide a new zest for living and working in the plans it generates.

If you decide to go this route in this run-through, one way to sensitize yourself to many "opportunity-type" challenges is to start out by making a cluster of wishes. Have a ball and let the child in you come out. Wish for anything and everything you want; you'll evaluate later. You may be surprised at what you'll generate if you really let go, defer all judgment and let the wishes flow. Even though some may seem ridiculous, the odds are that you'll find one desire that's manageable enough to work on realistically in a half-hour or so. This time you may feel better if you write your thoughts on something that you can destroy after you've selected the one you want to work on....

194

With whatever wish, dream or challenge you choose to work on, let's move through the process with just a reminder-summary of each step. If you should need more help in flowing with your thoughts, just go back to the appropriate step in the previous chapters for additional stimuli. If you chose "the big dream," you will need to break it down during the process into many bite-sized pieces. Deal with each element separately over an extended time-period so that you can turn the dream into reality.

FACT-FINDING:

1. List, sketch or symbolize as many facts and feelings as you can about whatever you have chosen. Who? What? When? Where? Why? How? VISUALIZE, DEFER JUDGMENT, FLOW!...

2. Did you flow? Did you use imagery? Did you record feelings? Review what you have written and underscore important elements that suggest problem-statements...

PROBLEM-FINDING:

1. Based on the data arrived at during Fact-Finding, list many questions starting with "In what ways might I...(IWWMI)?" Visualize, wish, ask "why?", find synonyms, etc. Keep recycling your resulting thoughts into new "IWWMI" questions. DEFER JUDGMENT! FLOW!....

The Saturday Evening Post
© 1958 The Curtis Publishing Company

"I've just made the most wonderful discovery."

2. Did you flow? Did you use imagery? Did you broaden and break down the problem? Now select the problem-statement you like best for creative attack...

IDEA-FINDING:

1. List, sketch or symbolize many ideas in response to your selected IWWMI question. Magnify, minify, rearrange. Visualize your ideas. Examine attributes. "force" relationships. DEFER JUDGMENT! FLOW!...

2. Did you flow? Did you use imagery? Choose the idea(s) you want to use first...

SOLUTION-FINDING:

1. List, sketch or symbolize many evaluative criteria: Effects on... Will it...? Visualize, empathize. DEFER JUDGMENT! FLOW!...

2. Did you flow? Did you use imagery? Glance over the criteria you recorded, underscoring those that you find especially important....

Momma

By Mell Lazarus

MOMMA by Mell Lazarus. Courtesy of Mell Lazarus and Field Newspaper Syndicate.

ACCEPTANCE-FINDING:

1. Use the criteria as tools to help you tailor your raw ideas into workable solutions. List, sketch or symbolize many ideas to help meet the challenges suggested by the criteria. Reshape, modify, adapt, magnify, minify, rearrange, combine, substitute. Fantasize! Visualize! List many who's, what's, where's, when's, why's, how's for gaining acceptance and implementing your ideas. DEFER JUDGMENT! FLOW!...

2. Did you flow? Did you use imagery? Now spell out a detailed plan. Visualize it taking place. Record new challenges of which you became aware and ways of dealing with these challenges. If the idea is quite difficult to implement, try the "30 Questions" checklist on page 189. Continue alternating with incubation....

THE NOW SOCIETY

Are you in the creative process or could you take
out the garbage?

Are You Going With the Probabilities?

Usually by applying the five-step process we break through to something worthwhile regarding our challenge or problem. When the "30 Questions" are used for additional flow in the Acceptance-finding step, the probabilities of arriving at something worthwhile are increased significantly. By alternating incubation with deliberate effort, the probabilities are increased even more. An aha is never guaranteed, but each time we allow for one more thought our chance of success is more probable.

Forcing relations between what we have recorded earlier and our current awareness also heightens the likelihood of achieving new ahas.

And the more we are willing and able to defer our decision while going through these processes, the greater the probability of a breakthrough to a better plan of action.

Are You Chipping Away?

The nature of the creative person can be dramatized by the story of the little boy who saw a sculptor beginning to work on a solid granite block. As he went by each day on his way to school, he paid little attention to the sculptor chipping away at the block. Then one day he suddenly noticed the emerging shape of a fully formed lion. "How did you know it was in there?" he asked the sculptor. The person working creatively "knows" it is there, and is willing to keep chipping away bit by bit until the solution emerges.

Michelangelo, while examining a piece of marble, reputedly said, "There is an angel imprisoned in it and I must set it free." We might say, "There is a solution frozen up in our minds, and we must melt it down and let it flow out." The procedures you have been exposed to in this book are designed to help that happen. Sometimes they help the problem itself melt away....

© 1967 United Feature Syndicate, Inc.

CHAPTER ELEVEN

All Set for Solo Flight?

Now, how about trying the process all by yourself? The following pages show only the names of the steps involved. Choose a new challenge, concern or idea, or something from your lists in Chapter 8 or 10.

Too often we deal only with problems that are blatantly in our way. An inordinate amount of time is spent "putting out fires" rather than structuring our lives so that fewer fires occur. We often cope in the sense of "I have to put up with it" instead of coping by visualizing, dreaming or foreseeing, and then dealing constructively with the vision. We allow ourselves to be controlled by our environment rather than being the controllers. We re-act rather than pro-act. We can create the problems, the mysteries, then solve them; or we can act only in the role of a detective, forever solving the mysteries or problems with which someone else confronts us.

If you are confronted by a pressing problem, then go with it and search for new ways of viewing and responding to it. Later perhaps you can try more of the "pro-acting" variety.

On the other hand, you might try for a challenge that you only sense or anticipate now. List a few like that, perhaps "wishes" that pop to mind, or use the first ten of the prompters again on page 143 to trigger a few additional ones. Then zero in on the one you'd like to use for this "solo" run-through.

Whatever the case, make your choice and go right on to Fact-finding on the next page....

THE FAMILY CIRCUS   By Bil Keane

"I have to write 50 facts for tomorrow. What's a fact?"

The family Circus by Bil Keane. Reprinted Courtesy The Register and Tribune Syndicate, Inc.

FACT-FINDING
(Data, including feelings)

Reprinted by permission of King Features Syndicate, Inc.

PROBLEM-FINDING
("In what ways might I..." definitions)

"I have to make a long distance call."

IDEA-FINDING
(Ideas)

THE FAMILY CIRCUS   By Bil Keane

8-11

"Wow! This is great! We really NEED this! First steady
rain we've had in weeks!"

SOLUTION-FINDING
(Criteria)

Tiger

Reprinted by permission of King Features Syndicate, Inc.

ACCEPTANCE-FINDING
(Implementation-ideas)

214

Perhaps your plan of action will only be a first step — "a juggling of one orange" or "doing one pushup." But, it can start a momentum that can grow and develop as you do more and more with additional ideas later. So, be sure to schedule into your plan a time to review the other thoughts you recorded. You may then "chip away," bit-by-bit, the broader issues involved....

Plan of Action:

New Challenges:

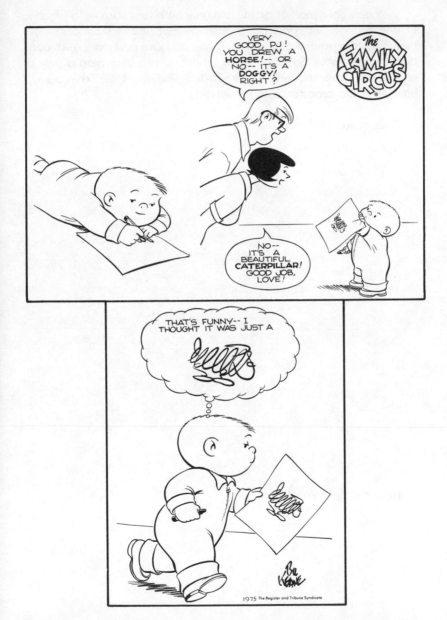

The family Circus by Bil Keane. Reprinted Courtesy The Register and Tribune Syndicate, Inc.

You might appreciate the touching reaction I once received to the "blank-page" type of session you just experienced in this chapter. It was from a partially-deaf student. Asked what she had gained from the session, she wrote, "Insight of what life is all about and that life to each individual is a blank page which only he can through experience fill; mostly he does it alone."

Our Drive for Ideas

It might be well to emphasize the relationship between learning creative problem-solving and learning to drive a car. When people first learn to drive, they are very conscious of each movement that is made with their hands and feet. After they have driven for a while, the movements become automatic — almost subconscious.

In working through this book, you have been learning to make certain "thinking movements" quite deliberately. Later you will probably find them to be subconscious — almost automatic. It will be as though you automatically make new connections and derive ahas in your problem-sensing and solving, not only by chance when "sleeping on it," but also when actively pursuing it mentally.

Let us extend the automobile analogy. When we first experience the full use of the process as in Chapter 8, it may be comparable to the first use of freeways in traveling cross-country. The super-highways provided unrestricted flow for long expanses, but then ended at large cities. We had to slow down to a snail's pace as we wound our way through city traffic. Likewise as you converged in the process at the end of each step, you may have found it very confining or frustrating to "slow down." Continuing the analogy, we now have city by-passes as part of our freeway system. We slow down only somewhat as we meet greater traffic around the city. Similarly, as you become more and more familiar and comfortable with the process, you learn to build your own "by-passes" and need slow down only slightly as you go from one step to another. The entire process then becomes smoother and more natural or comfortable, including your moving back and forth from deliberate to incubative effort....

Reprinted by permission of Ford Button.

CHAPTER TWELVE

Let's Really Emphasize Speed Thinking!

Let's speed up the process until it becomes internalized. We'll practice on some simple challenges like, "I'd enjoy concocting a new soup," or "I'd like to make the people at work feel good tomorrow." The following checklist may help trigger a variety of such challenges for you:

Family	Nutrition
Friends	Energy
Neighbors	Politics
Church	Health
Home	Recreation
Work	Purchases
Hobbies	Resources
Education	Finances
Transportation	Communication
Social Life	Technology
Sex	Aesthetics
Relationships	Retirement

Now choose one of those you thought of....

THE LOCKHORNS

3-28 Hoest

"LOOK AT IT THIS WAY········THERE ARE 364 DAYS IN THE YEAR THAT YOU <u>DON'T</u> HAVE TO CELEBRATE OUR ANNIVERSARY!"

Now, considering the challenge you selected, try spending only a few minutes on each step below.

FACT-FINDING:

1. Record the facts and feelings of the situation...

2. Visualize them as fully as you can; focus on the most significant...

PROBLEM-FINDING:

1. Record the "In What Ways Might I...(IWWMI)?" statements that come to mind. Keep rephrasing more IWWMI's as a result of answering "why?"...

2. Choose the statement that best reflects what you would like to accomplish at this moment. (Some statements may be good for later, more lengthy attacks.) Then fantasize accomplishing it, by magic if necessary....

The family Circus by Bil Keane. Reprinted Courtesy The Register and Tribune
Syndicate, Inc.

IDEA-FINDING:

1. Record ideas as fast as possible, using every technique you know, including visualizing, magnifying, minifying, rearranging, etc....

2. Select the idea(s) that intrigue you, the one(s) you like best...

SOLUTION-FINDING:

1. Record as many criteria as possible from as many different viewpoints as possible. Imagine yourself in others' skins...

2. Focus on the criteria you feel are most important, considering your own attitudes as well as those of others involved. Start adapting your idea to make it more workable, more manageable with respect to the criteria....

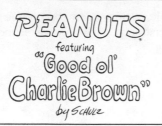

PEANUTS
featuring
"Good ol' Charlie Brown"
by SCHULZ

STRIKE TWO!

STRIKE THREE!

RATS!

I'LL NEVER BE A BIG-LEAGUE PLAYER! I JUST DON'T HAVE IT! ALL MY LIFE I'VE DREAMED OF PLAYING IN THE BIG LEAGUES, BUT I KNOW I'LL NEVER MAKE IT...

YOU'RE THINKING TOO FAR AHEAD, CHARLIE BROWN...WHAT YOU NEED TO DO IS TO SET YOURSELF MORE IMMEDIATE GOALS...

7-2

IMMEDIATE GOALS?

YES

START WITH THIS NEXT INNING WHEN YOU GO OUT TO PITCH...

SEE IF YOU CAN WALK OUT TO THE MOUND WITHOUT FALLING DOWN!

© 1972 United Feature Syndicate, Inc.

ACCEPTANCE-FINDING:

1. Record as many ways as possible to make your idea(s) work, to gain mutual acceptance, to get action. Visualize your ideas and keep revising them to meet the needs of your criteria, to add strength, to make the ideas more interesting or fun, etc....

2. Select your best implementation-ideas to work into a specific plan of action. What will be your first step within the next 24 hours?...What next?...Where?...How?...With whom?...Why?... Visualize it happening....

Action Plan:

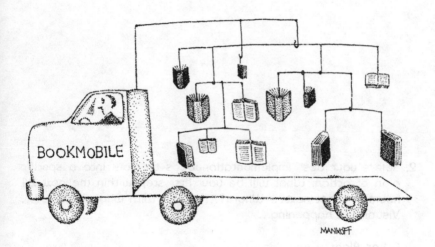

Reprinted with permission of Robert Mankoff and Saturday Review.

Do you have a plan that you feel good about? If not, try a bit of incubation. Then look back at your notes and see if anything new pops out. Repeat until you make some new connections that please you...

Try the process on several more "opportunity-type" challenges until you feel comfortable with the process and experience positive results more and more quickly. Once you are experiencing success, try compressing the process into less time for each step until you are doing the entire process in several minutes. Be sure to generate at least two or three thoughts under each step rather than merely the first thought...

Now try the same rapid process on an "obstacle-type" challenge like "I forgot to bring something home that my _____ is expecting" or "My secretary just handed me this poorly-typed letter that must be mailed today and he/she is ready to leave for the day." Make them simple challenges that need a decision quickly. List some of these below. Although they may not be earth-shaking, they can certainly make a difference....

228

Reprinted by permission of the Chicago Tribune-New York News Syndicate, Inc.

Select one of the challenges you listed and follow the same procedure as outlined on the previous pages. Limit yourself to a few
minutes per step:

- Fact-Finding
- Problem-Finding
- Idea-Finding
- Solution-Finding
- Acceptance-Finding
- Plan of Action

Now, choose another challenge from your list and try the process
again. Reduce the time you spend on each step. Do this gradually
until you are doing the entire process in a minute or so, with several
thoughts flowing under each step rather than only the first impulse
or "habit-thought." If you like, do it totally in your head without any
writing...

Prove to yourself that you can do the entire process in a very
short time when necessary; many problems in daily living have such
time constraints. But, when the situation warrants it, you can profit
by spending long blocks of time flowing with large numbers of
thoughts under each step. You be the judge as to how much time
you should spend in each situation. Remember, you can extend
your effectiveness by allowing incubation periods as much as possible before making final decisions. Work back and forth between
challenges, letting incubation take over when you remove your conscious attention. When you do so you increase the likelihood that
an important element buried in your memory may surface to your
consciousness. Be prepared always to capture it.

Dr. Lawrence Kubie, in his book, Neurotic Distortion of the Creative Process, tells of research where individuals were placed in a
strange room for a few minutes. After they left the room, they were
asked to list all the items they had seen there. The average person
listed 20-30 items. After being placed under hypnosis, however, the
same individuals then listed an average of about 200 more items!

Each of us has a deep well of knowledge buried in our mind; creative problem-solving involves many diverse processes to tap it and
apply it to our present concerns — beyond incubation alone....

DENNIS the MENACE

"I'M WAITIN' FOR A IDEA TO HIT ME."

By permission of Hank Ketcham and Field Enterprises Inc.

You probably know the five steps by heart now: Fact-finding, Problem-finding, Idea-finding, Solution-finding, Acceptance-finding. As a final challenge, you might want to walk through the process mentally in just a minute's time. Defer your immediate, impulsive, habitual, "prejudiced" response to a situation until you take a few moments to form new associations — to seek new viewpoints. You always have your habit response to fall back on, but chances are that you will discover some new element in one of the five steps that may make your response more effective.

Practice and more practice will enable you to change the habit of re-acting to something, to one of pro-acting. Whether deferring just long enough to make a snap decision without falling into the habit trap, or spending hours flowing through the process when appropriate, you are more likely to make a successful decision — while at the same time conditioning yourself to be always more comfortable and capable in meeting any new situation. Thus you develop increasing confidence that you can handle successfully whatever comes up in your life and work.

In creative problem-solving we capitalize on the deepest feasible search of the past as the springboard for a creative leap into the future. We strive to bring an ever greater amount of knowledge into working consciousness and interpolate it into projections of what might be. We then test these projections mentally. If and as our careful evaluation and development warrant, we then implement our new future.

Our Unbeatable Mind!

You may have read of the American prisoner-of-war who maintained his sanity during years of captivity and torture by deliberately exercising his imagination. He pictured himself building the dream house he wanted — room-by-room, brick-by-brick, nail-by-nail — until he had designed and built every square inch of the house in his mind. If, when being tortured, he lost the mental vision, he would begin all over again. His mind prevailed, and on his return to the United States, he built the dream house he had conceived.

Our mind can be our most powerful possession. It can discover our most exciting challenges, solve our toughest problems, and serve us when all else may seem to have failed. Don't ever lose sight of the "magic of your mind!"....

TYRANTS HAVE NOT YET
DISCOVERED ANY CHAINS
THAT CAN FETTER THE MIND.
... COLTON

footnotes

1. Ziv, A. The influence of humorous atmosphere on creativity. Unpublished manuscript, Tel Aviv University, 1980.
2. Parnes, S. J. & Noller, R. B. "Applied Creativity: The Creative Studies Project-Part II-Results of the Two-Year Program." Journal of Creative Behavior, 1972, 6(3).
3. Simberg, A. L. & Shannon, T. E. The effect of AC creativity training on the AC suggestion program. AC Spark Plug Division, General Motors Corporation (mimeo report, May 27, 1959).
4. Freud, S. The Basic Writings of Sigmund Freud, A. A. Brill (ed.). NYC: Random House, 1938, p. 193.
5. Noller, R. B., Parnes, S. J. & Biondi, A. M. Creative Actionbook. NYC: Scribners, 1976. (Adapted from pp. 112-113.)

References

For detailed information and theoretical background on the processes you have experienced in this book, the following annotated references are provided.

Parnes, S. J., Noller, R. B. & Biondi, A. M. Guide to Creative Action. NYC: Scribners, 1977. This is the most comprehensive of the references. Along with its companion Creative Actionbook, it serves as a "mini-encyclopedia" on the subject. It provides: (1) theoretical bases for creativity-development programs; (2) research summaries and references for studies referred to in the present book; (3) a detailed 225-hour instructional program for creativity development; (4) significant, representative readings on cultivating creative behavior; (5) hundreds of references on 75 methods, techniques and educational programs for stimulating creativity; (6) descriptions and sources of some 175 films on creativity; (7) hundreds of problems and exercises for creative thinking; (8) names, sources and references for some 100 testing instruments for studying creativity; (9) some 100 questions and topics for research; and (10) almost 2000 book references in the field of creative studies.

Parnes, S. J. "CPSI: The General System." Journal of Creative Behavior, 1977, 11 (1). This article provides a theoretical, general systems basis for the creative problem-solving processes of the present book. The Journal of Creative Behavior is a quarterly designed for the serious general reader in the field. It provides a continuous flow of pertinent information, research, developments, applications, literature, etc. It is published by the Creative Education Foundation, Inc., State University College at Buffalo, 1300 Elmwood Avenue, Chase Hall, Buffalo, New York 14222.

Parnes, S. J. Aha! Insights into Creative Behavior. Buffalo: D.O.K. Publications, 1975. This mini-book contains three articles: (1) The first was prepared for a stock-taking conference on research and developments in creativity for the 1950-1975 quarter-century. It includes a historical perspective of the development of the Creative Problem-Solving Institute program; also a discussion of how our balance of imagination and judgment relates to present-day developments in our culture. (2) The second article presents ways of applying creative approaches to problems of death and bereavement. It presents the challenge of turning these significant problems into opportunities. Thus it can serve as a prime example, in a most difficult area, of the present book's fundamental process of "opportunity-making." (3) The final article is a brief illustration of the use of the creative problem-solving process on a professional problem. (Applications of the process to diverse problems are also offered in the Creative Actionbook mentioned above. See Sessions 7, 9 and 12; also see the Special Supplement to Session 7 in the Guide to Creative Action, pp. 74-77.)